Praise for *She Believed HE Could, So She Did*

In her Christ-centered book, *She Believed HE Could, So She Did,* Becky Beresford reveals the truth of Jesus' sufficiency as we make Him preeminent in our lives. Not only does her book breathe hope to our souls, it breathes relief as well.

STASI ELDREDGE, bestselling author, *Captivating*

I've served in ministry for almost sixty years. Throughout that time, I've sought to empower God's daughters to be and do all God has created them for. Becky Beresford has given us a deeply scriptural guide for living empowered, not in the world's way of thinking, but in the courage and humility of walking with and learning from Jesus. One by one she exposes the lies the world feeds us and reveals transforming truths from God Himself.

JUDY DOUGLASS, speaker, author, encourager, Global Director for Cru's Women's Resources

Many of us race through life while feeling anxious and overwhelmed. We believe the lie that if we just try harder and believe in ourselves more, *THEN* we will overcome. It's an impossible standard to keep up with. In *She Believed HE Could, So She Did,* Becky shines a light on how to live a life of *TRUE* Christ-centered freedom by relying on God alone for our strength and sufficiency! I'm so relieved this message is out for all of us women to hear and embrace!

AMY FORD, founder and president of *Embrace Grace*; author of *Help Her Be Brave: Discover Your Place in the Pro-Life Movement*

Society and the enemy have lied to us. We've believed these false narratives for far too long, and it's time to discover the truth. With biblical wisdom and courage, Becky Beresford challenges and changes our perspectives on ourselves and God. Through her book *She Believed HE Could, So She Did,* Becky is leading the charge to proclaim the freedom of the gospel. This book will transform you and change our culture. Get ready to believe and live differently.

RACHAEL ADAMS, author of *A Little Goes a Long Way* and host of *The Love Offering* podcast

Today's world is full of half-truths that are supposed to make us feel better about ourselves and our abilities but only end up making us feel inadequate, exhausted, and burned out. I am so guilty of this myself! But in *She Believed HE Could, So She Did,* Becky reminds us why these common sayings are actually lies and offers us an alternative through gospel truth. We are God's daughters who can stand strong in who He created us to be. This is a book to read time and time again so you can be continually reminded of your God-given identity and be empowered to change the world around you with His strength.

STEPH THURLING, coauthor of *Raising Prayerful Kids*; Executive Director of Christian Parenting

We live in a culture that espouses, "If it's going to be, it's up to me." That is a burden many of my patients (and I) have carried that was never meant to be ours to carry. If we could make the world spin through our own efforts, we never would have needed a Savior who promised to carry our burdens. The choice is ours whether or not to cast our cares on Him. But striving to achieve every next thing in our own strength is exhausting. Take Becky's hand, learn from her transparent sharing of her struggles and victories, avow to stop "should-ing" on yourself, and experience the freedom that comes when we let God do the heavy lifting. You'll be thankful you did!

> **MICHELLE BENGTSON,** Board Certified Clinical Neuropsychologist, host of *Your Hope Filled Perspective* podcast, and award-winning author of several books, including *The Hem of His Garment: Reaching Out to God When Pain Overwhelms*

If you are exhausted from culture's recipes for self-reliance, pick up this book. It is filled with gospel-centered encouragement that, by Christ's strength, you can be free of the lie that you must do more to earn favor or approval. As a recovering achiever with the fear of failure, Becky's words were a balm to my heart. I know they will offer the same to you!

> **REBECCA GEORGE,** author of *Do the Thing: Gospel-Centered Goals, Gumption, and Grace for the Go-Getter Girl* and host of the *Radical Radiance* podcast

There is something undeniably powerful about a woman who knows exactly who she is not, because she is confident in who and *whose* she is. In Becky's beautifully counter-cultural book, women are invited to dismantle the lies they've believed and throw off the stress of striving by anchoring in their Christ-centered identities as beloved daughters of God. In a society where we are constantly pushed toward self-reliance, this is the message of liberation and authentic empowerment that we desperately need to hear.

> **JENNY ERLINGSSON,** speaker and author of *Becoming His: Finding Your Place as a Daughter of God* and *Her Part to Play*

There are lots of feel-good affirmations out there that are meant to soothe and inspire us—sayings like "You be you" and "Follow your heart." The problem is they're not based on truth. In *She Believed HE Could, So She Did,* Becky Beresford takes a countercultural approach to these assertions that push women toward perfectionism and performance-based approval and holds those beliefs against a biblical construct. Ultimately, our worth is found in the person of Jesus Christ, who loved, honored, defended, and respected women. Beresford's book will help readers understand their worth is based not on a crazy works-and-looks scale but instead in their Savior. I highly recommend this book!

> **JANET HOLM MCHENRY,** award-winning speaker and bestselling author of 26 books, including *PrayerWalk, The Complete Guide to the Prayers of Jesus,* and *Praying Personalities*

Becky is a bold and courageous writer! I love how she trades in lies for what God actually says in *She Believed HE Could, So She Did.* Today's culture needs truth and not compromise. Becky conquers the enemy in this timely read!

> **COURTNAYE RICHARD,** speaker, author, podcast host, founder of Inside Out with Courtnaye

she believed HE could, so she did

TRADING CULTURE'S LIES FOR CHRIST-CENTERED EMPOWERMENT

BECKY BERESFORD

MOODY PUBLISHERS
CHICAGO

All emphasis in Scripture has been added.

Edited by Cheryl Molin
Interior design: Ragont Design
Cover design: Erik M. Peterson

Library of Congress Cataloging-in-Publication Data

Names: Beresford, Becky, author.
Title: She believed He could, so she did : trading culture's lies for
Christ-centered empowerment / Becky Beresford.
Description: Chicago : Moody Publishers, [2024] | Includes bibliographical
references. | Summary: "Our culture tells us lies. Lies about female
empowerment within our world. Becky Beresford knows because she once
believed and even promoted some of these lies. But in God's kindness,
Becky came to the end of herself. And that is when she was able to
embrace life-giving and healing truth found in the Bible. Tired and
frustrated with self-dependence, Becky longs to be God-dependent. And
she invites you to join her on this journey. In She Believed HE Could So
She Did, Becky dismantles commonly held misconceptions and lies so we
can live in real freedom and truth. Women, this is a journey toward
freedom as we learn to experience Christ-centered empowerment-not by
believing in ourselves . . . but by trusting in our faithful God"--
Provided by publisher.
Identifiers: LCCN 2023031827 (print) | LCCN 2023031828 (ebook) | ISBN
9780802429988 (paperback) | ISBN 9780802473400 (ebook)
Subjects: LCSH: Christian women--Religious life. | Christian women--Conduct
of life. | Feminism--Religious aspects--Christianity. | BISAC: RELIGION
/ Christian Living / Women's Interests | RELIGION / Christian Living /
Personal Growth
Classification: LCC BV4527 .B4539 2024 (print) | LCC BV4527 (ebook) | DDC
248.8/43--dc23/eng/20231020
LC record available at https://lccn.loc.gov/2023031827
LC ebook record available at https://lccn.loc.gov/2023031828

Originally delivered by fleets of horse-drawn wagons, the affordable paperbacks from D. L. Moody's publishing house resourced the church and served everyday people. Now, after more than 125 years of publishing and ministry, Moody Publishers' mission remains the same—even if our delivery systems have changed a bit. For more information on other books (and resources) created from a biblical perspective, go to www.moodypublishers.com or write to:

Moody Publishers
820 N. LaSalle Boulevard
Chicago, IL 60610

1 3 5 7 9 10 8 6 4 2

Printed in the United States of America

To the woman who wants to let Jesus be the Savior of her story,
may you experience true freedom found in the gospel.

To my husband and wonderful sons, you are my treasures.
Thank you for all you've sacrificed to make this book possible.
May you always believe in the God who can.

CONTENTS

Introduction 9

PART 1: ***She Believed HE Could . . . Trading Culture's Lies for Christ-Centered Empowerment***

Chapter 1: ~~You Are Enough~~ You're Not Enough, and That's the Good News 19

Chapter 2: ~~You Can Do Hard Things~~ You Can Do Hard Things the Easier Way 31

Chapter 3: ~~You Be You~~ You Be His 43

Chapter 4: ~~Believe in Yourself~~ Believe in Your God 55

Chapter 5: ~~Speak Your Truth~~ Share Your Story, but Speak THE Truth 71

Chapter 6: ~~Follow Your Heart~~ Follow Your King 85

Chapter 7: ~~The Future Is Female~~ The Future Is Found Together 97

PART 2: ***. . . So She Did. Living Out the Truths of the Gospel in Christ***

Chapter 8: You Can Slay All Day 113

Chapter 9: We Are Women of the Way: Spreading the Gospel Like Jesus 127

Chapter 10: How to Put the Enemy in His Place (Part 1): Understanding the Enemy 141

Chapter 11: How to Put the Enemy in His Place (Part 2): Undoing the Enemy 153

Chapter 12: What to Do with Our God-Given Rights 171

Chapter 13: Cultivating Holy Courage in a Harsh World 185

Appendix 197

Acknowledgments 211

Notes 217

Introduction

HOW CAN FEMALE EMPOWERMENT START WITH A MAN?

A few years ago, God put it on my heart to write an apology letter to my readers. I tried to reason with Him and see if there was another way to tell these women what needed to be said, but it was clear. This was something I had to do.

For years I had one goal in ministry: point women to Jesus and help them walk closely with Him. I wanted to empower women and help them be bold daughters doing important kingdom work. Yet, somewhere along the way, an undercurrent of lies began to seep into my writing. I was dishing out small doses of deception, unaware I wasn't telling the whole truth. That is . . . until Jesus set me free.

It all started with a sign. Literally.

My husband bought it from Hobby Lobby when I decided to push past my fears and call myself a writer. In simple white letters it read *She Believed She Could, So She Did*. I'd seen the phrase everywhere, plastered on cute mugs and shirts and journals. Clearly, I wasn't the only one who was drawn to this saying. I wanted to believe in the potential and promise of these words. I told myself if I only had more faith in my self-made grit, I could achieve whatever God wanted me to achieve and be whoever He wanted me to be. I could handle whatever life threw my way; all I had to do was be strong and believe.

So, when my marriage teetered on the brink of divorce, I tried to believe I could.

When my autistic son needed help recovering from another meltdown, I tried to believe I could.

When my body was shutting down from intense anxiety and overwhelm, I tried to believe I could.

Except I faced a growing problem. *No matter how hard I tried to believe in myself, I still felt like a failure. I actually didn't think I could.* Sure, on the outside I could pretend I was holding the fragmented parts of my story together, but inside my heart kept telling me I was a disappointment for continually messing up.

One day while I was looking at the sign on my desk, the words stared back at me, almost teasing me for trying. A chasm of confusion and pain expanded between us. What was I missing? Why was this saying not sitting right anymore?

In that moment, the Holy Spirit revealed something that changed my life. I was free, but I wasn't experiencing Christ-centered freedom. Galatians 5:1 says, "For freedom Christ has set us free; stand firm therefore, and do not submit again to a yoke of slavery" (ESV). Here I was, trying to live according to society's version of empowerment for women, yet I was enslaved to a lie—*a false gospel.* My feelings of failure and confusion were not the problem, because they could point me to Jesus. But something was wrong with the saying.

I grabbed a black marker and immediately colored over one white letter on the sign. As I stared at the words again, the new phrase made my spirit feel light.

She Believed HE Could, So She Did.

One letter removed made everything right.

I couldn't help but wonder, how many other women were believing this lie, living out an impossible narrative given to them by a world preaching self-reliance and personal power? How many believers were feeding a perspective that pushed perfectionism and rewarded performance? God had nudged me to write an apology, and soon the apology grew into the contents of this book.

I apologized for not pointing my fellow sisters toward the saving power of relying on God alone for strength and sufficiency. I apologized for watering down the gospel with culture's mediocre Kool-Aid. I had unknowingly jumped on the spinning wheels of the wrong bandwagon, and I was sorry. But not anymore.

Since writing the apology letter, I received an overwhelming response from women who felt the same way I did. Not only did this message resonate with my readers, but also I realized God's women were sick of it.

Women were done being lied to, done being told what empowerment should look like without considering the Bible, done looking *inward* when their spirits were pointing them *upward*.

We are sick of being self-dependent.

We want to be God-dependent.

And we want that journey to start now.

How Can Female Empowerment Start with a Man?

As I began to do research for this book, it shocked me how much culture's definition of female empowerment has infiltrated our beliefs about God and ourselves. Let me ask you a question. Have you heard any of these popular phrases preached in our culture, but also in Christian circles?

You are enough.

You can do hard things.

Believe in yourself.

Speak your truth.

You be you.

Follow your heart.

The future is female.

All familiar sayings. All seem well-intentioned and inspiring. Yet *none are found in the Bible.*

This may be surprising, but trust me, the environment we encounter as women has been well crafted since Eden. The enemy of our souls has done a fantastic job taking the Savior out of our stories. All of these ideologies have removed Christ and His cross from the scope of the picture, making it all about us, not Him. When the ultimate Empowerer is eliminated from the equation, we set women up for an inferior form of empowerment that leaves them feeling like failures instead of favored daughters.

When I first became a blogger, I used to encourage my sisters in Christ with these exact cultural phrases. Granted, I had a fear of rejection and need for approval that made me shy away from anything controversial or possibly hurtful. It felt safe to let women know what was right with them, to make them feel good about themselves without any mention of weakness or sin. My heart still does not want to cause pain or offend.

But when I look at the ministry of Jesus, He was never afraid to say what was true because truth leads to freedom. And freedom leads to life.

So are you ready? Because here is the glorious truth, the solitary certainty our Savior died to give:

We are enough—*in Jesus.*

We can do hard things—*through Christ who strengthens us.*

We shouldn't believe in ourselves, but instead, *should rely on the power and sufficiency of our capable God,* who can accomplish far more than anything we could imagine or dream.

We were never made to conquer it all by ourselves—we can't and never could. We are not able to be perfect in this life—we aren't and don't need to put on an act. It's okay if we let our flaws show. In fact, recognizing our weaknesses as a child of God shouldn't lead to shame, but to strength.

Paul wrote in 2 Corinthians 12:9–10, "But he said to me, 'My grace is sufficient for you, for *my power is made perfect in weakness.*' Therefore I will boast all the more gladly of my weaknesses, so that *the power of Christ may rest upon me.* For the sake of Christ, then, I am content with weaknesses, insults, hardships, persecutions, and calamities. For when I am weak, then I am strong" (ESV).

What if we were content with our weaknesses, welcoming them instead of avoiding them? What if our feelings of failure actually ushered in a sacred falling away—an undoing of our own strength and a yielding to our King's? This new mindset would bring freedom in its purest form and help us experience grace as it's meant to be.

But before we see the fruit of freedom, lies need to be dismantled. Women need to be fed the correct narrative, one filtered through the lens of God's Word. As it turns out, true empowerment has never been about us. It doesn't even start with a woman.

Female empowerment starts with a man, and His name is Jesus Christ.

Female Empowerment Was God's Idea First

The Son of God was interested in raising up His sisters, more than anyone else in history. The Bible says Jesus came to destroy the works of the devil (1 John 3:8). We can see the outworking of the fall, when sin became a part of humanity's story, and the consequences have been pushed along by Satan ever since. The ripple effect has created disconnection in our relationship with God and friction between men and women (more on that a bit later). But the Author of our lives is not simply rewriting what was decreed over us; He is restoring what was lost and stolen. God is bringing us back to our original design, back to who we were in the garden, except now the outcome is even more glorious.

When we think of the Trinity—God the Father, Jesus the Son, and the Holy Spirit—*they are the strongest united force in empowering women and supporting their equal standing to men.*

Jesus' interaction with women when doing kingdom work always reflected restoring their value as well as their God-given rights. This was extremely countercultural. We in the Western Hemisphere are far removed from the context of the Bible and the significance that came from having women followers and disciples. It's normal to us. But back then, women were treated like second-class citizens.[1] To even speak to a woman in public if you were a man meant you were willing to go against the societal grain. The way Jesus openly interacted with women was radical.

Many of us are familiar with the sisters Martha and Mary. Martha invited Jesus and His followers over to her house and started cooking a large meal to provide warm hospitality. Cooking and hospitality are not my gifts, so we can give Martha her well-earned props. But soon she gets frustrated when she realizes her sister, Mary, is *sitting at Jesus' feet* listening to His teaching, instead of serving Him in the home like she is. Martha walks into the room, calls out Mary for how unfair it is, and tells Jesus to make her help. His response?

"But the Lord said to her, 'My dear Martha, you are worried and upset over all these details! There is only one thing worth being concerned about. Mary has discovered it, and it will not be taken away from her'" (Luke 10:41–42).

What is this mysterious one thing Mary has discovered? First, we need to dig a little deeper.

Mary was sitting at the feet of Jesus. Although women were not officially prevented from sitting in this position, it was very uncommon for a woman to sit where the rabbi's male students were usually seated. This spot was reserved for disciples—for those learning from the master, eager to follow his ways. Mary was acknowledging Jesus' lordship, but He was acknowledging her role and importance. She was equal to men in God's sight and just as precious in significance.

Mary had discovered true intimacy with Christ, but she had also discovered His acceptance and approval of her inherent worth.

What God has given to His daughters cannot be taken away by anyone else. It's true for Mary. And it's true for us all.

A Brave Invitation to Experience Christ-Centered Empowerment

If this is the heart of our Savior, then coming under His care and capacity should not be a problem, right? I wish that were the case, but the answer is a hearty no!

Our world has done an incredible job of persuading us that Jesus is not enough. We've been told the burden to thrive is at our feet and it's up to us to get the care we need. We've become the savior of our own stories. Meanwhile, we walk around with burdens bearing down on our bodies and souls, wondering how we will take another step. This is not the way our loving Father wants us to live.

The heartbeat behind our God is love and *freedom*. It's also the message of this book.

These pages will be an invitation to experience loving freedom when we let go and lean in to the steadfast faithfulness of our Father. It's a call to trust in God's ability instead of our own—to believe He can, so that...

We will believe in His promises.

We will believe in the beauty of the gospel.

We will believe what the Bible says versus the philosophies of the world.

Within these pages, we will:

- Break down cultural ideologies around female empowerment and bring them before the unchanging Word of God.
- Look at God's heart for women and disentangle the enemy's lies used to ensnare our souls.
- Learn how to put the enemy in his place and live boldly as a disciple of Jesus.
- Examine our true purpose and discover how we can live empowered by Christ in tangible ways. Right where we are. Right now.

Because this message resonates with women worldwide, including their voices within these pages is vital. At the end of each chapter you will find a short personal story from fellow sisters *who believed God could.* Discussion questions are included for deeper connection with Jesus, as well as connection within community. This transformative journey is meant to be taken together.

I am only one woman empowered by Christ. It takes a revolution to change the cultural tide. It takes a multitude to win a war. With God on our side, it's a battle that has already been won, but we have the privilege of walking that victory out. Let's link arms and move forward in freedom as one. The true gospel is alive and waiting.

This is your invitation, Brave Reader.

Are you in?

Part 1:

She Believed HE Could . . .

Trading Culture's Lies for Christ-Centered Empowerment

Chapter 1

~~YOU ARE ENOUGH~~ YOU'RE NOT ENOUGH, AND THAT'S THE GOOD NEWS

"I'll never be enough for you!" I yelled as I slammed our bedroom door.

In reality, I never felt like I was enough for anyone, let alone my husband. We were about a decade into our marriage and our relationship was accelerating toward the threshold of separation. As someone who struggled with pleasing people her whole life, feeling like I could not do enough to save our marriage or help my husband heal from trauma was gut-wrenching.

I wanted to fix things. I wanted to paint myself as a perfect wife. I wanted to forgive and move forward, but bitterness had planted its fatal root and I was ashamed for letting it happen. Blame bled into the deepest part of my heart, leaving me knee-deep in guilt. Day after day, *I could barely handle the pain.* No matter how hard I tried, I couldn't get out of this pit to bandage my own wounds.

Until recently, when I would fight with my husband, I'd roam around our bedroom and turn the pictures of us face down on the tables. Yes, I was usually angry. And yes, I'd leave them that way so he could see it. Not my finest hours, but my hurt feelings were often doing the leading. What I didn't realize was that every time I hid a photo from his sight and mine, I allowed myself to be swallowed by shame. I couldn't look at those pictures because I saw how my husband was caring for me, and how could anyone love me when I acted foolishly or said those awful words? How could my flaws be covered when my failure seemed too great?

People know me as an encourager. And yet, the same tongue that speaks life also whispers death, and it can be potent when someone is hurting, especially for the ones we love.

We all have ugly parts of our lives we don't want others to see or know.

Well, now you know one of mine . . . and I'm glad. A little squeamish, but glad. And here's why. Telling our full story (ugly bits and all) ushers in the gift of authenticity, but it also creates needed space where others can see God's redemption.

How Can My Lack Lead to Something Good?

"Has the LORD redeemed you? Then speak out!
  Tell others he has redeemed you from your enemies."
(Ps. 107:2)

In the moments when darkness hovers thickly, we need to remember two important things:

(1) Nobody is too far gone from the redemptive hand of God.

(2) We have an enemy who fights against all that is good.

The word *gospel* comes from the Anglo-Saxon term *god-spell*, meaning "good story." It's a translation of the Latin word *evangelium* and the

Greek word *euangelion,* meaning "good news" or "good telling."[1] At its core, the gospel is the ultimate story of God's redemption, taking all that the enemy meant for evil and turning it around for good. But what does this mean for us when we feel weak or powerless?

It means everything.

We worship a God who chose us from before the foundation of the world, knowing who we were, what we would do, and where we would go. And yet, the love He has for His children outweighs the heaviest of costs, even the death of His Son on a cross. The gospel is good not because of what we have or haven't done—rather, the gospel is good because the Maker of heaven and earth has done everything *for* us.

This *good story* points toward our desperate need for God and highlights His extravagant act of deliverance. It shows how we cannot depend on ourselves, we cannot save ourselves, we cannot dig our way out of the muck and the mire. We are in too deep. And so, our Father "reached down from heaven and rescued [us]; he drew [us] out of deep waters" (Ps. 18:16). When we are drowning or wish the raging waves would still, God becomes our rescue. He is both our salvation and our continual lifesaver.

Power is present as we share our honest stories, when we let others know we are *not* enough, and we never want to be—not when there is One who is more than enough for all. With every declaration of God's ability to redeem our struggles, we offer up our lives as a glorious retelling of the good news.

We get to show others how absence in our life ushers in His abundance. How our failings give God the opportunity to fill. How our lessening on earth means we experience the kingdom's gain.

Today when I say I'm not enough, I feel a sense of release. I've been liberated from the pressure to please or the drive to earn my own worth. *I can't be enough for my husband* because that is Christ's role alone to fill. *My husband can't be enough for me* because only Christ can be my all.

Jesus is the single source of sufficiency and security that can satisfy the empty parts of every human soul. There are no exceptions, no matter what society may tell us.

Only the cross can wash away our sins, and only in our weaknesses can we be made new and whole—not by our efforts or hard-won grit, but by the gracious love of the Father who promises to make us complete in the fullness of Himself.

Can you say this sentence with me? And please, say it with audacity and boldness.

I am not enough, but the Great I AM is enough for me.

And repeat.

This is the key to walking empowered. And it's the truth Satan has tried to steal.

Why'd You Have to Be So Cruel? The Targeted Assault on Eve

We will be going back to the garden of Eden a few more times in this book, but have you ever wondered why Satan went after Eve first?

To be clear, we can't actually know. But it's a question I've thought about often. In Stasi Eldredge's book *Captivating,* she talks about a "special hatred" Satan has for women, which made him choose Eve before Adam.

> The message of our wounds nearly always is, "This is because of you. This is what you deserve." It changes things to realize that, no, it is because you are *glorious* that these things happened. It is because you are powerful. It is because you are a major threat to the kingdom of darkness. Because you uniquely carry the glory of God to the world.
>
> You are hated *because* of your beauty and power.[2]

Two things are happening here. It's possible Satan despised Eve because he was tremendously jealous of her God-given beauty, both physically and spiritually. He hated the way she represented the heart of God. Some believe Satan used to be the most glorious of all God's creation before he fell into pride and sin. But now . . . he's *not*. Humanity will always take the cake.

Moreover, Satan was terrified of her potential to destroy his plans. Earlier in the chapter, Eldredge says:

> Eve is his greatest human threat, for she brings life. She is a life-saver and a life giver. Eve means "life" or "life producer." . . . Put those two things together—that Eve incarnates the Beauty of God and she gives life to the world. Satan's bitter heart cannot bear it. He assaults her with a special hatred.[3]

Women were too much of a threat for the prince of darkness. Clearly, Eve had to go. And what's the first thing Satan tried to do?

He made her forget who she already was.

After placing a seed of doubt regarding God's kind character, the crafty serpent went in for the literal kill, lying about the consequences of Eve's actions, but he also added something more malignant. He said, "For God knows that when you eat of it your eyes will be opened, *and you will be like God,* knowing good and evil" (Gen. 3:5 ESV).

Satan makes it plain as day. He tells Eve she is lacking—*she is not enough, so she must do something else to make herself more.* He wants Eve to believe God is withholding because then she would decide to reach for something extra in order to attain what she already had. Satan wants Eve to take matters into her own hands and independently make herself like God, not just His beautiful image bearer. This is the same lethal lie our current culture has adopted. It's the same hidden poison attacking the Father's hurting daughters today.

The enemy wanted Eve to feel like she was incomplete and imperfect *because* she was already complete and perfect in God. But after she took the first bite, she experienced a separation between her spirit and the fullness of her Creator, and the falsehood whispered in her ear became a fixed reality. It was a cruel and harsh self-fulfilling prophecy. She didn't believe she was enough, but she only stepped into lacking when she chose to separate herself from God. Eve chose an inferior form of empowerment.

Listen closely, sister. *The enemy's greatest strategy is to keep women from going back to their Maker and walking in the care and capacity of Christ.* Eve needs to remember God is enough, which means as she walks in His sufficiency, she will always be enough in Him.

But the forces of hell are scared we will find out. When Christian women know *whose* they are and *who* fills their entire being, they become a threat so powerful, the devil's knees begin to shake.

Enough with Enough

I've experienced pushback from Christians as I've communicated the fact that we aren't enough over the years. Many say there's biblical backing for claiming we are enough. So I ask for the verses they are talking about, because if I have missed something, I really do want to know. And guess what?

Not one person can find the phrase in the Bible.

Instead, they give verses declaring our worth in Jesus and how deeply we are loved. They talk about being fearfully and wonderfully made in the image of God and how we are called "good" in the garden. They mention feeling seen and known by the Father when others dismiss them. Or they point toward the grace and gentleness of Christ, not His condemnation, as conduits for transformation. And to all of this I say YES! I agree with every one of these biblical truths. But where in

Scripture does it say the specific phrase *we are enough*?

It doesn't, because being *enough* implies something else completely.

Here are two definitions for the word *enough*: (1) "As much as is necessary; in the amount or to the degree needed."[4] (2) "Occurring in such quantity, quality, or scope as to fully meet demands, needs, or expectations."[5] Fully meeting the list of demands? Satisfying every need and expectation? Proclaiming my "enoughness" as the measure of what is necessary in order to tackle all situations, for all people? Do I really think I am enough, therefore changing anything or accepting help is unwarranted because I can fulfill the entirety of my needs? Am I really okay on my own?

In short, saying we are enough is equivalent to saying we don't need anything else, including a Savior.

This may not be our intention or what we really mean, but when we use this phrase we are falling into the same trap Satan set for Eve. We are letting God know we are enough on our own and we don't need any assistance from Him. We are trying to be adequate apart from Jesus, taking the bait to empower ourselves by being like God. The enemy wants us to think we are enough because then we are less likely to reach out for the Father's hand and will choose the fruit instead.

I find it interesting that we can communicate our feelings and scripturally sound beliefs like the ones mentioned above without saying we are enough. We can say "I am loved" or "I am valuable" or "I am accepted in Christ." We can say these simple and true statements, but we don't because talking ourselves into believing and saying we are enough implies more and unknowingly adds lies into the mix.

Declaring ourselves as enough only reiterates culture's narrative that everything is dependent on you and about you. Thankfully, because of God's grace and kindness, it's not! Circumstances and your identity are dependent on Christ because He will be more than enough for you and me, which makes us more than enough in Him. It's time we say *enough* to being enough.

Be the Real Eve

I want to end this chapter by looking at the one word this book will continue to come back to: *empowerment.*

According to *Merriam-Webster*, the definition of empowerment is as follows: "The act or action of empowering someone or something: the granting of the power, right, or authority to perform various acts or duties."[6]

A granting of power.

A giving of rights.

An imparting of authority.

All of which are bestowed upon someone from on high.

Transferred from the top down.

Here on earth as it is in heaven.

The garden was God's original plan played out on earth. Authority and power were the birthrights of His beloved children as they walked by His side in love. And yet, Adam and Eve chose to believe a cunning creature over their Creator God. They chose to believe in themselves over the faithfulness of the One who formed them by hand.

But we have a choice too. We can choose to veer away from Adam and Eve's fallen footsteps and follow the path back to a restored identity in Christ. We can choose to believe God's Word and trade the enemy's lies for the Father's irreversible promises.

Will we still encounter sin? Of course. Will we still see the ripple effects of the fall, including the vicious assault on women? Unfortunately, yes.

But clinging to falsehood will not help women grow or overcome. The "you are enough" ideology is not the answer to empowering women. It's society's attempt to counter the lies of Satan and make right what went wrong in Eden. When we continually try to be enough for everyone, including ourselves, we will eventually realize we can't be our own Messiah. And that's okay because there's good news. *Only Jesus can do what we can't.*

Only Jesus can take our condemnation and cover us with His grace.

Only Jesus can take our lack and make it a holy gain.

Only Jesus can use our weakness as an outlet for His strength.

Only Jesus can free our hearts from the pressure of perfection.

Only Jesus can make us enough, because we are united in Him.

Without the restorative, healing work of Christ in our lives, we will end up trying to earn our worth through an unending cycle of defeat. We will wear our bones dry trying to prove our self-sufficiency through the power of our own hands. We can work. We can volunteer. We can be moms. We can be wives. We can run the schedule. We can create the perfect home. We can pursue the dream. We can be the good neighbor, churchgoer, daughter, sister, and friend. But when we mess up or can't get past the struggle or can't keep our head above the sand, we can expect another spiritual assault from the enemy.

Satan will tell you it's your fault and pack on loads of shame. *He will do everything he can to make you forget the position you've been given.* But don't let him fool you. Don't let him make you feel inferior when in Christ your identity stands.

The truth is, we are worthy of being cherished and accepted simply because we are His. We can receive the Father's compassion exactly where we are, and it's not because of what we do or who we try to be. Our value has already been determined by the good story of the gospel. Our position has been sealed and our inheritance guaranteed.

God made up His mind about us long ago, and the verdict is eternally in.

He wants to be with us. He wants to show His faithfulness. He wants to walk in paradise with those He calls His friends. We don't need to reach for anything else that extends beyond God.

And so, dear reader, may I leave you with one of the most empowering and encouraging passages in Scripture?

> I pray that from his glorious, unlimited resources *he will empower you* with inner strength through his Spirit. Then Christ will make his home in your hearts as you trust in him. Your roots will grow down into God's love and keep you strong. And may you have the power to understand, as all God's people should, how wide, how long, how high, and how deep his love is. May you experience the love of Christ, though it is too great to understand fully. Then you will be made complete with *all the fullness of life and power that comes from God*. (Eph. 3:16–19)

In Christ, we lack nothing. We are made whole and complete by the extravagance of His love. In Jesus, we are empowered, filled to the fullness of life and power that comes from the throne room of God. We aren't enough on our own, and that's okay. It's actually a relief. We can say we are more than enough through the One who covers us in His perfection and offers us His peace.

So, the next time the devil tries to slither his way into your mind, do the one thing he hates the most. Stand a little taller and claim who you *already* are.

Be you.

Be the real Eve.

Stories from Sisters Who Believed HE Could

JEN'S STORY:

In 2021, I was diagnosed with peripheral neuropathy, a disorder characterized by damage to the nerves that presents as pain, tingling, and numbness. After years of my seeking treatments, the Spirit challenged me to replace my incessant search for answers with a wholehearted search for the deeper things of God.

I began praying for a fresh infilling of the Holy Spirit and shared this with a friend. One morning after church, her husband approached me and said, "I know what you're praying for, and I want you to know I'm praying alongside you." He told me he had a life-altering encounter with the Spirit at a revival service years prior, unaware that I'd been invited to one that evening. I considered this confirmation that I was supposed to attend.

During the sermon, the Lord brought to my mind the story of Jacob wrestling with God. I, too, was desperate for more of Him. I needed God's blessing and strength to sustain me through chronic pain. Clothed with holy confidence, I approached the altar with those who were receiving the gift of salvation and asked for prayer.

I had a personal experience with God that night. The Spirit's presence was tangible, and I sought His direction regarding what to do next. I felt He wanted me to taper off the pain medication I'd become dependent on, so I took a step of faith, knowing I couldn't do it on my own. He would have to be enough for me. While this decision was solely between the Lord and me (and is not reflective of everyone's journey with health issues), God was faithful to provide.

He not only strengthened me to endure my pain without

medication, God also gave me the strength to begin serving others who were suffering. My entire ministry pivoted to serving those in pain, in order to reveal the nature of Christ. His abundant grace is sufficient to equip us for what He's called us to do, especially when we are at our weakest. Our greatest contributions to the kingdom are not achieved through our own power but His. (*Jen R. from Maryland*)

Chapter 2

~~YOU CAN DO HARD THINGS~~ YOU CAN DO HARD THINGS THE EASIER WAY

This past Mother's Day, my youngest son gave me the most adorable plant holder made out of rainbow popsicle sticks. He and his classmates worked hard on crafting their gifts, and as a bonus, they included a pretty planted flower in the holder. My boy beamed with joy as he handed it to me.

"Make sure you don't kill it, Mom. The teacher says you need to water it each day."

I smiled nervously, knowing what was about to happen. Unlike the rest of my immediate family, God did not bestow on me a green-thumb gene. My mother's gardens are glorious. She creates sanctuaries of serenity that give us a glimpse into the beauty of Eden. Meanwhile, I've killed almost every plant we've purchased.

I was determined to keep this flower alive, and also my child's hope in his plant-challenged mother. I watered it multiple times a day and placed it in open sunlight on the windowsill. But as the days carried on, the flower began to wilt. I'd *over*watered it. My mind flashed back to the summer before when I spent five hours trimming our bushes with scissors. Later that day my mom once again proved her gardening intelligence and told me they had a hedger that could've accomplished the job in a few minutes. My aching body wanted to cry.

What comes naturally to some can be hard for others, and sometimes we can make things much harder than God wants them to be.

We Live in a Tired World

Not long ago, I conducted a survey with women in my life who follow Jesus. I asked a simple question: *What are some phrases you've heard that make you feel empowered?*

One of the top answers was *You Can Do Hard Things*. And on the surface level, we can. God has made His daughters strong in multiple ways. But what happens when we peek just below the surface of our own efforts? What happens when we look at the inner workings of our hearts as we face the hardships of life head-on?

The answer can be summed up in one sentence: *We find a world of weary women.*

We grow weary from pushing and pulling and prying to make things happen. We feel tired after using every ounce of energy we have to serve those we love. We're exhausted in the depths of our aching bones because we've taken on too much and now we're worn too thin.

It's a tricky business, doing hard things. Many women come to accept the normalcy of being weary because what we are striving to do is often simultaneously hard and good. Being weary becomes worth it. We were made to do good for the glory of God's kingdom, but should it be at the expense of barely surviving or feeling like we can't breathe? Sometimes we can wear weariness like a badge of honor because weariness proves we are doing all we possibly can. But according to the God of rest, we may be doing hard things in a much harder way.

If our noble efforts are left unchecked by the Holy Spirit, endless acts of service can lead to shame-filled burnout. Holy passion without the power of God behind it is still performance. And performing for Christ cannot coexist with His peace if we are going at our preconceived fast pace.

We need to slow our stride down.

Reducing our desire to serve, achieve, or overcome may not be the answer. But increasing our willingness to listen is. When we lessen our pace, we slow our steps in order to match our Savior's. We allow our souls to remain still in order to hear from God and follow His direction because He knows an easier, Spirit-led way.

From one resolute woman to another, resting in God's ability will always bring the best results. While we definitely need physical rest, developing a heart that trusts in what God can accomplish is a must.

Life is rarely easy breezy. Winds rage. Storms surge. We are told trouble will be entwined into our earthly days. Jesus said to His disciples, "I have told you all this so that you may have peace in me. Here on earth you will have many trials and sorrows. But take heart, because I have overcome the world" (John 16:33). We will have many chances to do hard things and we want to do them well. Our determination can become detrimental, however, when we depend on ourselves instead of God for deliverance from our difficulties. Sometimes there's just too much to handle.

When Life's Too Hard to Handle

If you hang around Christian circles long enough, you will hear the popular phrase: "God will never give you more than you can handle."

I used to believe this too, until I realized God must think I can handle *a lot* and it didn't seem fair. But again, we come to another idea that has been taken out of context and is nonexistent in Scripture.

Many people who hold this belief quote 1 Corinthians 10:13, where Paul writes to the Corinthian church, "The temptations in your life are no different from what others experience. And God is faithful. He will not allow the temptation to be more than you can stand. When you are tempted, he will show you a way out so that you can endure." The apostle is assuring them God will help them resist sin, not that He wouldn't give them more hard things than they could handle.

God was letting them and us know that when believers encounter sinful temptations, God will help us endure it by giving us a way out of the temptation through the power of the Holy Spirit. Even Jesus experienced a temptation to sin but He didn't yield to it. If Paul meant God will never give us more than we can handle, then he would be contradicting himself later when he wrote a second letter to the church at Corinth.

Paul says, "We think you ought to know, dear brothers and sisters, about the trouble we went through in the province of Asia. We were crushed and overwhelmed *beyond our ability to endure,* and we thought we would never live through it. In fact, we expected to die. But as a result, we stopped relying on ourselves and *learned to rely only on God,* who raises the dead" (2 Cor. 1:8–9).

What faith Paul has! They were past the ability to endure and even thought they were going to die. Yet, these trials were catalysts to help them learn how to rely on God. Paul ends by expressing his confidence that God could raise them from the dead if it was His will.

The Lord allows hard situations to happen in our lives, many being more than we can handle, in order to emphasize His faithfulness to save. If we could handle it all, why would we need Jesus? It's in the moments when we are too weak that God's greatness shines through. God's Word makes a countercultural correlation between weakness and strength—one Paul was very familiar with.

The apostle shared about asking God three times to take away a form of affliction that was challenging, even tormenting. But God continued to allow the difficulty to carry on and it wasn't without purpose. Paul said the Lord's response was, "My grace is sufficient for you, for my power is made perfect in weakness" (2 Cor. 12:9 ESV). This switched Paul's attitude from resenting his weaknesses to boasting about them in order to let Christ's power rest within him. In God's economy being weak brings about strength, because Christ's power enables us to do every hard thing.

So, the next time you feel like you've been given more than you can handle, remember, no amount of girl power can compare to God's power. We can face the there's-no-way-I'm-going-to-make-it conditions with assurance. Jesus will be our rescue. When troubles are more than we can hold, let's hand them back to Him.

What God's Strength Is Meant For

A common verse we turn to when facing hard times is Philippians 4:13, "I can do all things through Christ who strengthens me" (NKJV). It's such an inspiring verse, but it's also been misused.

Paul is talking to fellow Christians in Philippi, thanking them for giving toward his needs. But Paul puts a little twist in his message and tells his brothers and sisters he has never truly been in need because he has learned to be content in every physical circumstance, with little or plenty. Immediately following this explanation, Paul pens this famous verse. But he makes sure to highlight how Christ has made it possible for him to face these hard, varying circumstances.

Many people believe this verse means God will help them do whatever they set their minds to. However, when read in context, this verse is saying God will empower us to face whatever situation *He allows us to walk through*. There's a big difference.

We can have aspirations God is not behind. This can be a little shocking, right? Just because we want something doesn't mean God will bring it into being. Human ambition and aspiration need to be aligned with God's objective and Word.

Being a follower of Christ is not about achieving our goals or even getting what we desire. Instead, it involves relying on God when we are in want and being grateful when we have plenty. If our efforts have left us frayed and we can't push through anymore, that's when our God will give us the strength to sustain and succeed according to His plan.

The beautiful thing about letting God strengthen us is that we don't have to wait until we get to the end of our floundering rope to experience His help. Everything doesn't have to be going haywire to have God step in. We can come to the end of ourselves without being sucked dry, and it's done through the posture of release.

Muscle contractions are a good example. When we tighten our muscles, we can feel the tension. But unless you have the supernatural ability to hold your muscle in that same contraction for hours on end, your body will get tired and the muscle will loosen as you experience release. Our body comes to a state of rest when we release our cares to Jesus. If we choose to tighten our grip and never let go of the worries, fears, and feelings troubling us, we'll remain in a state of rigid overwhelm. Releasing everything into the trustworthy grip of God will help us move from a place of pressure to a posture of peace.

Discerning What God Wants Us to Do

If you are a fellow over-committer like me, let's breathe a long sigh of solidarity together. I get you, my friend. Whether it's because we have a fear of missing out or we want to serve or maybe we just love being with community, often there's no shortage of projects or activities we can do. If we want to be a part of all the action but we're exhausted, stepping away is truly an act of faith.

Circumstances get more challenging when we are asked to help and we don't want to let others down or leave them in a bind. We want to be responsible and reliable people. And we really don't want to hurt others' feelings or make matters worse. But when did it become our duty to do all the *doing*? God didn't assign us this task. When we look at the Bible, God is the One who establishes outcomes and He decides what's best for His kids.

We want to avoid being helpers who do too much and then feel helpless.

Evaluating our weary hearts and bodies is a good way to be honest with ourselves and our Maker. If weariness begins to take over, we need to ask ourselves if the roles we are performing are God-assigned or self-appointed. And if we've appointed ourselves without God's anointed wisdom or guidance, we need to take the initiative and let some of it go. We need to learn the art of saying no.

Feeling guilty should not be part of creating boundaries, but it too often is. We may feel bad for not being able to be there for others the way we always have. But saying no is an opportunity to trust God with those we love. It's a tangible demonstration of our faith in God because we believe He can do the things we can't. He also excels at the things we think we can do on our own. At the end of the day, we aren't here on earth to do what people want us to do. We are here to accomplish what God wants us to do, and we don't need to feel bad about that.

Not everyone has the same budget for doing. Some people, like myself, have less margin for taking on tasks or responsibilities because their mental load is full from life's heavy situations. We are a special-needs family, which means our home is anything but pristine. Still, I can't tell you how many times I've compared my home to the neat, cute homes of friends. I return from their houses and start "guilt cleaning" with plenty of huffs in tow. Thankfully, Jesus values perseverance over perfection.

We *all* face struggles. No one has a flawless family. Nobody has an eternally immaculate home. Social media delivers a message of perfection, but for the sake of all that is holy, we need to stop scrolling and worshiping a standard that doesn't exist. It's not healthy for our heads or hearts.

By taking this needed stance, we are also releasing ourselves, as well as others, from the pressure to perform. When we decide to stop striving to be the perfect version of ourselves, we say *yes* and *thank you* to the full gospel. People we encounter suddenly become those who are valuable and capable of receiving God's most precious gift—salvation by grace and faith alone.

As God's daughters we are given what we don't deserve (grace) and we are spared from what we should receive (mercy). It's definitely a win-win! But if we try to add our own efforts back into the picture or we expect others to do the same, we actually detract from the fulfillment of the good news.

Paul says, "My old self has been crucified with Christ. It is no longer I who live, but Christ lives in me. So I live in this earthly body by trusting in the Son of God, who loved me and gave himself for me. *I do not treat the grace of God as meaningless.* For if keeping the law could make us right with God, then there was no need for Christ to die" (Gal. 2:20–21).

A little later he adds, "After starting your new lives in the Spirit, why are you now trying to become perfect by your own human effort? Have you experienced so much for nothing? Surely it was not in vain, was it? I ask you again, does God give you the Holy Spirit and work miracles among you because you obey the law? Of course not! *It is because you believe the message you heard about Christ*" (Gal. 3:3–5).

We are perfect in Christ because we believed He could.

Before we do, we first need to believe He did. It's not about us or our power or our packed schedules. The world doesn't need more weary women. It needs wise women who rely on God's guidance and rest in His care. God's grace is not meaningless when we give Him control of our daily decisions and trust in the foundational facts of the cross.

We don't do more in order to be like Christ. We seek Christ and then He will show us what to do.

The Root of It All

I started this chapter with the woes of gardening and my anti-green thumb. The themes of planting, farming, and trees are scattered throughout the Bible, but there's more to these themes than being something everyone can culturally relate to.

Trees are used for their symbolism. So much meaning lies behind how they are grown. In the previous chapter, we looked at Ephesians 3:17–18: "Your roots will grow down into God's love and keep you strong. And may you have the power to understand, as all God's people should, how wide, how long, how high, and how deep his love is."

Roots are fundamental in determining a tree's strength. It's not about the height of the tree or its width. It's not about the lushness of its leaves or the vast amount of fruit it produces. What matters the most is how deep and secure its roots are. How deep do *we* go?

When looking at this verse more intently, we find Paul is talking about the range and depth of the roots we have in Jesus. Christ's love is our strength and the true outpouring of our empowerment. We can try to root our power in ourselves, but when the winds come by force, without solid roots in our Savior, our efforts will snap. They will break into pieces and we will be left scavenging through piles of our limited self-sufficiency.

Jesus is our ultimate Root. He is the root of Jesse referenced in

Isaiah 11:10, "In that day the root of Jesse, who shall stand as a signal for the peoples—of him shall the nations inquire, and his resting place shall be glorious" (ESV). The idea of resting in Christ creates an opportunity for us to rely on His capacity, which results in glory, not for ourselves but for God.

Our Father is also the wisest Gardener. He knows how to tend the soil. He knows what needs to be pruned. He knows what needs to be done in order to make us more grounded in Him, even if it pushes us outside our comfort zone.

Did you know harsh winds are actually necessary for trees to grow resilient roots and make them tower tall? Dennis Merritt Jones reported about an important experiment done in a biodome in the desert years ago. Scientists grew trees, but they would only grow to a certain height before they fell to the ground. Experts couldn't figure it out until they realized they had created the perfect environment for growth, with the exception of wind. There was no outside force pushing against the trees to foster the roots' growth, which in turn would have helped support the trees as they grew taller and matured.[1]

Resistance is needed to grow resilience.

The hardships that come against us in life are used by our God, who knows the better way, if we allow Him to have control. God's good purpose will win out. No pain will ever be wasted. Instead, our strength and determination will be forged through the fires as we trust that Jesus will not let us be consumed by the flames.

"But blessed is the one who trusts in the LORD, whose confidence is in him. They will be like a tree planted by the water that sends out its roots by the stream. It does not fear when heat comes; its leaves are always green. It has no worries in a year of drought and never fails to bear fruit" (Jer. 17:7–8 NIV). We are evergreen with God's blessing because our confidence is in Christ and our roots are firmly planted in His love. Life is not immune from trials or difficulties, but rough conditions can produce resilience and rooted trust in God.

May we flourish into the strong women God is empowering us to be, no matter the soil, no matter how hard the winds blow.

Would you look at that? Maybe I enjoy gardening after all.

Stories from Sisters Who Believed HE Could

TERESA'S STORY:

Parenting is challenging. Nurturing children genuinely and selflessly requires more sacrifice and intention than I had anticipated. It requires constant outpouring, attentiveness, problem-solving, and flexibility. As the daily demands of motherhood slowly chipped away at my seemingly patient demeanor, it was uncomfortable and I didn't adapt well to this loss of independence.

God had gifted me parenthood, charging me to navigate this challenging journey with Him. But my irritability often opposed His work. I ignored the deeper problem and persisted while we decided to become foster parents. I exhausted myself in pouring out from my already taxed and limited love, which ironically made me centered on self.

By God's grace, I was allowed to burn out. I crumbled emotionally, becoming anxious and short-tempered. In weariness, resentment grew toward anyone who needed me. No amount of self-care could ease the exhaustion or warm the fire in my heart.

I brought my years of struggles to the cross, the safest place I know. Confessing my selfishness, I submitted myself to the gospel again. I grieved, repented, and received unlimited forgiveness. Ultimately, foster parenting remained at the altar. We discontinued a foster adoption and grieved that loss for more than a year. It was a vulnerable place, sacrificing a ministry and feeling disqualified because of my weakness. Yet Jesus continually tended to my wounds, washed away my old attitudes, and renewed my mind. He also filled my heart.

Now I truly parent from a Christ-centered perspective. I acknowledge my need of God's love and power for every good and hard work. Having resolved to serve from God's heart and strength, I thrive in the empowerment of Christ. Beautifully, He has recommissioned the ministry of foster parenting and I know He'll enable me to do the hard work ahead sourced from His limitless love and strength. (*Teresa L. from Texas*)

Chapter 3

~~YOU BE YOU~~
YOU BE HIS

I have a pair of shoes in my closet that I absolutely love, but apparently they do not love me. They're the perfect black pair. You know, the ones that go with any outfit. I got them on sale even though they were a half size too small simply because I have a mental block against buying expensive shoes. My feet, however, are informing me I need to get over my hang-up.

Before purchasing these adorable shoes, I tried to rationalize how it could work. I wanted them to fit, so I told rational Becky to calm down because surely we could stretch them out. But even after years of trying to "break them in," they give me blisters every time I wear them and usually result in an aching back. My feet are smashed into shoes that don't fit because of my stubborn determination to make them work. Denying the size of my feet used to be worth the discomfort, but now I can no longer deal with the painful toll they take on my toes and body. These shoes deserve to be worn by someone else because (and I say this with sadness) they were not made for me.

Why am I telling you all of this? (1) I need to bite the bullet and buy new quality shoes, and (2) God sees us when we are trying to be something we are not and He wants to offer us freedom.

All too often we try to fit into a mold we were never made to fit. Whether it's shoes, clothes, personalities, lifestyles, beliefs, or choices, we can easily get wrapped up in the expectations of others, including ourselves.

That's why I understand the meaning behind the common expression *You be you* and its attempt to encourage us. I support part of this message. Nobody should try to force themselves into a mold their Maker did not craft for them. You can't be me and, no matter how hard I try, I will never be you. We are unique individuals. This is a healthy and holy stance for approaching life.

The red flags start to rise when we take this beautiful form of diversity, meant to glorify the many facets of God, and try to define ourselves according to our *own* desires and standards. Our identity stops being founded on Jesus and instead becomes tied to who we think we should be.

As we've established before, culture is trying to take Christ out of creation. Therefore, when people say, "You be you," they are not basing this sentiment on Scripture. Instead, this mentality gives us permission to be the best version of ourselves, not unique Spirit-filled reflections of God's Son.

But what is the best version of myself? This definition is extremely subjective, changing with the tide of society's trends and the opinions of others. When I think about all the things I wanted to be while growing up, they changed almost every year.

I had an undecided major in college until my junior year. When I graduated I still didn't know how God would use my Communications degree. I didn't know who I really was because I was just discovering the ways God designed me. And honestly, I'm still figuring out what God has planned as I grow older. "Being me" has been a journey, but being me without remembering who I am in Jesus puts me in jeopardy.

The real risk of remaining in the *you be you* mindset without being centered on Christ is that our perspective can easily detach from biblical truths regarding our personhood. If we take the reins and determine who we should be without listening to God's definition, our beliefs and decisions can venture outside of His design for our lives. When we turn away from what God has for us, He's gracious and won't force us to become more like Jesus or acknowledge who we are in Christ. He may let us take the harder route, even if the path we choose is painful and perilous, before we finally acknowledge Him and come home.

I think about prodigal sons and daughters. The ones who choose to do life according to their own terms. As parents, we don't want to see them get hurt, especially when they are hurting themselves. In the Bible the prodigal son would rather have his father dead so he could receive his inheritance early, to do whatever he'd like with what was "rightfully his."

How often do we pursue our "entitlements" to passions, plans, and pleasures that promise happiness but actually prevent us from experiencing the presence of God who fills us with purpose and worth?

After wasting the inheritance given to him, the prodigal realizes what he's lost: not only possessions but also his relationship with his father and his identity as part of that family. The son has forgotten who he is—the child of a faithful, heartbroken father whose unconditional love has driven him to search the road daily for his son. The father desperately waits for his return like God longs for us to return to a relationship with Him.

Even before repentance enters the picture, the father still recognizes the value of his son because the prodigal remains connected to the father through the bond of family. Similarly, God sees us and has fashioned us to display His image and heart to the world—to represent His family well—even if we, as His children, can't see it yet ourselves. God knows us better than we know ourselves.

The Bible says, "For God knew his people in advance, and he chose them to become like his Son, so that his Son would be the firstborn among many brothers and sisters. And having chosen them, he called them to come to him. And having called them, he gave them right standing with himself. And having given them right standing, he gave them his glory" (Rom. 8:29–30).

We were chosen and called to be like Christ because the Father has given us right standing with Himself through the cross. We were not created to be mediocre self-made versions of who we think we should be; we've been given God's glory! And yet, when we drift away it gets harder and harder to hear our Father's voice. Soon other voices begin to beckon us, and sometimes we listen to the wrong ones.

Listening to the Right Voices

There will never be scarcity in the number of voices telling us what to do.

We don't have regular cable in our house. We have some techy thing my husband set up that lets us access certain channels we want to watch, which means we get to avoid the bombardment of ads and mass media. Praise God.

It's exhausting watching television and its surge of voices flooding our minds with what they think we should do or become. Most care more about making a profit than profiting us for the good. They persuade and push, not provide and protect. With so many voices lingering in the air, we need to focus on God's intentionality. His is the only one we should continually entertain and trust, and that includes not trusting ourselves.

I want to make it clear that I am not saying we shouldn't ever trust our gut, although many times it's actually the Holy Spirit giving us a needed nudge. I'm also not saying we don't have knowledge about what is happening with our minds, hearts, and bodies. God has given us the ability to be sensitive to what is going on within so we can turn to Him for help and wisdom. But we shouldn't always listen to our own voice, especially if it sounds like something the enemy would say or contradicts God's Word.

Other than Satan, we are often our own worst enemy. The critical voice inside our heads can make us rip ourselves to shreds. Negative self-talk seeps into our spirits, perhaps echoing someone's harsh words from our past. Regardless of how the voices got there, the effect is still the same. If we're not careful, we will begin to listen to what's being said, sometimes on repeat.

There's a difference between hearing and listening. Hearing is the literal "process, function, or power of perceiving sound."[1] Listening, on the other hand, involves considering what's been laid out on the table. It places interest in the words one is hearing. Listening can lead to welcoming ideas, inviting them into our hearts, minds, and ultimately our actions.

This distinction should make us pause. We may be hearing the voice of God, but are we actually listening? Are we taking in what God communicates through Scripture, the Spirit, and even other wise believers? Because while the Shepherd is calling out to His sheep, the enemy will be as wolfish as he can be. He will distract and discourage in an attempt to prevent us from following Jesus and representing His likeness in our own special ways.

One way Satan does this is by planting destructive seeds of jealousy in our minds, making us long for more *this* or at least some more of *that.* The enemy doesn't want us to be content with how we were created. He wants us to compare, critique, and compete with others. What better way to break down the body of Christ than to have the body tear itself apart?

Comparison is a covert compromiser of relationships. It's often silent but still has serious consequences. We compare jean sizes, jobs, families, spouses, houses, and things. But it goes even deeper. We can also play the comparison game with each other's God-given abilities, which are meant to develop the kingdom, not build barriers that harbor bitter feelings. These gifts of the Spirit have been intricately woven into our being by God, but they end up becoming a threat or a discouragement when seen through the eyes of envy.

Ready for the good news? We have a way out of this prison of discontentment. We can break free from comparison by *practicing the art of celebration.*

When we're grateful for how others are made, we can celebrate their distinct makeup instead of wishing their brains, bodies, or circumstances were ours. We can come alongside our sisters and partner with them in their giftings. Creating an environment of collaboration is a sure way to stop comparison in its tracks.

God values celebration and collaboration over comparison. He says we are to "rejoice with those who rejoice, weep with those who weep" (Rom. 12:15 ESV). Ephesians talks about the beauty of diversity found within believers. Paul says, "He makes the whole body fit together perfectly. As each part does its own special work, it helps the other parts grow, so that the whole body is healthy and growing and full of love" (Eph. 4:16). Like a well-planned puzzle, celebration is a conduit through which the body of Christ shows joy-filled support and binds itself together in love. Celebration promotes unity and wholeness instead of partnering with the enemy's attempts to destroy and divide. Celebrating others shows we understand God's heart and we are choosing to listen to His voice above the rest.

Getting Rid of the Worst Cousins Around

You be you has a not-too-distant cousin named *You do you.* The cousins may sound cute together, but trust me, they make a nasty pair. Another way of describing them is *be who you want* and *do what you please.* For those of us who struggle with comparison or people-pleasing (raising my hand high!), this definition can be revised even more to say *be like them* and *do what others want*. Either version of these popular phrases does not align with God's commands, and it certainly isn't found in the Bible.

Caring about what others think is a real struggle, or at least it was for me. The common saying "sticks and stones will break my bones, but words will never hurt me" is just not true. Words wound. Accusations and insults hurt. It takes me a good chunk of time to get over harsh words that have been hurled in my direction.

But Jesus has helped me release these painful situations to Him. Although people may have a negative outlook about who I am, their opinions do not define me. I am not dependent on the approval of humanity. No one's opinion matters more than Christ's because nobody has done more for me than He has. We are forever indebted out of gratitude.

"But now, this is what the LORD says, He who is your Creator, Jacob, and He who formed you, Israel: 'Do not fear, for I have redeemed you; I have called you by name; you are Mine!'" (Isa. 43:1 NASB). We are not our own. Yes, we always have free will, by which we are called to live as new creations. But the moment we decide to believe in Jesus and surrender our lives over into His love-scarred hands, we release our perceived control to God and invite Him into every part of our being.

As the apostle Paul says, "Don't you realize that your body is the temple of the Holy Spirit, who lives in you and was given to you by God? You do not belong to yourself, for God bought you with a high price" (1 Cor. 6:19–20). That price was the sacrificed blood of Christ, a price the Father was willing to pay in order to have us by His side. It was the most expensive payment God could have ever paid because restoration cost Him the most precious thing—His beloved Son.

I have three boys. I make sure to hug them each day and call them my treasures. I memorize the looks in their eyes, the dimples on their cheeks, and the smiles on their faces. To think of willingly choosing to let one of them die for the sake of another is something I can't even fathom. I would rather die than have anything happen to them.

But God's love is just that—*unfathomable.* It surpasses understanding and goes past our knowledge. Why would God give up His Son, knowing the vast majority of the world would reject Him? Why would He allow His heart to break, recognizing many would not want to be in a relationship with Him? There is no logical answer but love.

They say love is blind, but God's eyes were wide open when He made the choice to sacrifice His Son. *He knew the cost to make us His.*

So many times we casually say God loves us. But do we really let those words sink in? Do we let the full weight of what it means to have someone want us so deeply soak into our very souls? Once we do, all we can do is lay down our lives and thank Him.

This kind of sacrifice was not done in order to empower us to do whatever we want or be whoever we want to be. God is interested in every detail of our lives and He will establish our steps as we rely on His guidance and leading. God's plans bring about a hope and future if we are willing to posture our hearts and ask, *Lord, who do You want me to be?*

You Were Made for This

Now that we've kicked *you do you* to the curb, how about we get to the good stuff. You were not made by accident. When the Creator of the universe crafted your being, He made you with purpose and precision, all the way down to the God-given longings and talents He built into your being. No one can represent God's image in the exact way you can.

Have you ever sat down and made a list of what makes you come alive? What brings you joy? Is there something others say you do well? It's wise to take note, because while we need to make sure our aspirations are aligned with our Maker's, God wants us to discover the desires He has placed within.

I was talking with my youngest boy, Ben, the other day and he said something that struck me to the core. A little context for you: my son is an artist. And by artist, I mean he lives and breathes creating, drawing, painting, and sculpting. My cleaning skills can't keep up with his creativity. Most days our house looks like an art museum exploded.

Ben had a class project that needed to be completed, so I bought some yarn for him, thinking he could use it for hair or something similar. Before I knew it, he had used the yarn to make a perfectly shaped 3D Yoshi with eyes glued on it and everything. He was six, my friend. I couldn't do this as a fortysomething!

When he was almost finished making his creation, he looked up at me and said, "Mommy, am I a good artist?"

"Of course you are, buddy! You're an amazing artist. So talented."

He smiled and nodded. Then he stunned me. "*Yeah, I was made for this.*"

I wanted to borrow some of his confidence. Could someone so young know exactly what he was made for, even before he could spell? His clarity shook me in the best way. What if we embraced how God has formed and fashioned us instead of excusing ourselves from participating? Can you imagine a world full of women who, in their own unique ways and with their specific gifts, boldly proclaim Christ? It would be a powerful sight to behold.

And yet, we often question how God has made us. We shake our heads when God tells us to step into our callings because clearly, He must be talking to the wrong girl. We see our flaws and imperfections as disqualifications or derailments from being used by God as part of His kingdom. We need to work on ourselves first before we go about God's work. And while, yes, God is constantly transforming us into the image of Christ, He does not have a prerequisite of perfection in order for us to walk in our purpose.

Think about Moses. He stammered in his speech. And yet, God called him to be a mouthpiece of freedom for Israel. Abram and Sarai (later renamed Abraham and Sarah) could not have children. And yet,

God promised they would be the ancestors of God's people who are too numerous to count. Ruth was a widowed foreigner. And yet, God called her to be in the lineage of Jesus, the Restorer who would make outcasts know they truly belong.

If God is doing the calling, He will do the equipping.

Fear may try to rob us of the joy we'll feel when we know we're right where God wants us to be. Fear is just a freezing agent. It keeps us from believing in God and His ability to use us as He wills. We don't need to worry about whether we can do it, whatever "it" may be. That is God's responsibility. The outcomes continually remain in His court.

Our Father doesn't ask us to be flawless in order to follow His plan. He doesn't see our weaknesses as something to be feared. He sees our willingness as something to be formed. Christ asked His disciples for a commitment to the commission and calling He'd placed on their lives.

We shouldn't ask "Who, me?" when we hear God's call. Why *not* you? Like Christ's early followers, when our Savior stretches out His arm, He invites us on the journey with the words *come and see*. What an adventure it will be to see what God will do through you!

The Beauty of Belonging

I want to revisit a verse from earlier in this chapter because I have a confession to make. The Bible says, "You do not belong to yourself, for God bought you with a high price" (1 Cor. 6:19–20). I used to shy away from this verse until I realized the beauty behind it. While the thought of belonging to someone else besides ourselves may make us pause, the idea of having someone to belong to outweighs the hesitation. We are not foreigners to Jesus. We belong to the family of God. He knows us. He sees every part of our lives and hears every cry we send toward heaven. Nothing about us goes unnoticed by Him because we are significant to the Savior.

Like the father with his prodigal son, God cares more about us as children than the success of carrying out our callings. Likewise, similar to the father with his self-righteous son (the prodigal's brother), God doesn't love us because of what we do, even when we are doing things for Him. We are covered, protected, and provided for simply because we belong to the family of God. We can allow ourselves to be cared for by Jesus.

We can rely on our efforts in order to find a place to belong. We can try to create our own identity. Or we can allow Christ to gift us His. The terms "in Christ," "in the Lord," and "in him" occur 164 times in Paul's letters, making this the most common description in the Bible of a follower of Jesus.[2] We are united to Christ. When the Father looks at us He sees we belong to His Son, which means we will always have a place to call home. It also means we will inherit the benefits of being a child of God.

As an heir of the King, we have access to His kingdom. We are saints who can still struggle with sin, but we are also God's royal ones who reign through the righteousness of Jesus. Our spirits begin to shift away from the world's pleasures, passions, or possessions because all we need can be found in Christ.

There's nothing like knowing we belong to the Father. The price He paid is irreversible, which means it's a security that will carry on and last. May our hearts rest in this safe space.

We are God's.

He is ours.

Now *that* is a perfect fit.

Stories from Sisters Who Believed HE Could

SHAWNA'S STORY:

The train from the Upper East Side to Grand Central Station emptied like ants running from an intruder. The rush of weekday commuters consistently invigorated my aspirations and quickened my pace. My pride soared as my heels clicked along the sidewalk and through the building up to my thirtieth floor office with coffee in hand. *This is the life I was designed to live,* I thought to myself.

Five years later I exchanged my heels for sneakers and business lunches for toddler playdates. Meanwhile, my heart doubted the purpose of it all: my degree, my gifts, my significance. Joy waned as I constantly fought the belief that my life was on hold. Had I forfeited the life I was designed to live when I left the corporate world to stay home and raise children?

The constant desire for something else to satisfy my endless longings was exhausting. Over time and with abundant grace, God revealed that the life I truly desired was not found in pursuing performance as my identity or comparison as my assurance, but by faithfully embracing life one day at a time. God opened my eyes to see His purpose in the diverse gifts He entrusted to me to steward—not to build my own kingdom, but to build up His greater kingdom. With my unique gifts, experiences, and desires, I discovered that lasting joy comes from simply being His regardless of title or achievement.

What joy might we discover when we say yes to His unchanging purpose for us over our constant performance? As we say yes to what God has for us, may we uncover the beauty of each season, the diversity of our gifts, and the wonders of His everlasting love. It's the life we are all designed to live. (*Shawna S. from Texas*)

Chapter 4

~~BELIEVE IN YOURSELF~~

BELIEVE IN YOUR GOD

On a perfect summer evening, when everything seemed in control, I came home from my son's baseball practice only to discover our sweet golden retriever, Callie, was missing. No one knew how long she'd been gone, but our entire family frantically darted into the car, half of us without shoes. The sun was beginning to set, and coyotes commonly roamed the long stretches of cornfields behind our neighborhood. We knew our time to search was short.

The search started with just us, but soon family, friends, and many kind souls from our neighborhood were out looking for our dog before darkness took over the surrounding farmland. It seemed like an impossible feat. Neighbors said they saw Callie darting out into the cornfields, but no one had spotted her since.

My heart and stomach were in knots. Thinking about her alone at night made me feel sick. Callie was my dog. Golden retrievers love their families, but anyone who's owned a dog knows they usually pick one human as their favorite. Callie chose me. I was the blessed one she'd look for and follow everywhere. Now my shadow was gone, leaving a gaping hole in our family.

For four hours, our boys and I called Callie's name into the night through the rolled-down windows of our SUV. At one point I pulled over, unable to stop myself from breaking down in front of my kids. A sweet stranger who lived in our neighborhood drove up behind me and asked if I was looking for the dog too. Once she saw we were "the family," she offered us her flashlight and promised to keep searching. She told us she couldn't imagine how we felt since they had a dog they really loved too.

Up until that night, we hadn't felt connected to our neighborhood. Being a special-needs family can be very isolating. But as the countless cars took to the streets, we saw the tangible outpouring of God's comfort from these people who were His hands and feet when we needed them most. Together we prayed, looked, and waited.

We didn't find Callie that night. Or the next.

No one reported a single sighting of our dog for two days, even though we did all we could. We put up posters, handed out flyers, drove on all the local roads, and walked through nearby woods.

We posted on social media, called animal shelters, and checked with vets. We put her bedding on the porch and laid dirty laundry across the front railing in hopes she would be drawn to a familiar smell. We walked our other dog where she went missing and let him mark to his heart's content. We tried everything, and still there was no word from anyone.

Truth be told, we were powerless to bring her back. We didn't know where she was, if she was alive, or what would make her come out of hiding.

No matter how much we tried or how much we believed our efforts would result in a happy ending, ultimately God would have to bring our girl home. Only the Maker could work out the impossible.

Have you been here too? Like me, have you whispered a desperate plea into the night—*God, only You can do this.*

At some point everyone will encounter an "only God" moment. It's the eye-opening realization that we've done everything we can, and yet we can't change what is happening. We've run out of ideas, resources, or skills and all that's left is to trust and wait.

Yet in this uncomfortable space a necessary unraveling starts to take place. We begin to see how the message of this world doesn't align with our actual experience. We try to put our trust in what we can do, but life shows us that believing in ourselves is not always enough. Depending on our dependability does not guarantee security or success. And while this disconnect makes us feel uneasy, God wants us to linger here in order to understand what's true.

The Father knows we'll confront raging fires and battles far too big for us to fight on our own, which means "believing in me" is not the best option. Culture's idea of self-faith is fragile when played out in the long run. Walking with God is an *eternal* journey, so we need to make sure we are trusting in the One whose dependability will last.

When we believe the gospel, we are choosing to believe in something bigger than what we can produce. We exchange believing in *ourselves* for believing in our *God*. Following Jesus was never meant to be about having faith in the followers, and that includes following ourselves. If we start trusting in someone more than Christ for our worth, security, and empowerment, we will venture into unsteady, and often ugly, territory.

This isn't anything new. Many early Christians struggled with aligning themselves to well-known disciples instead of tethering their hearts to Christ. Paul had some strong words to say about this.

> When one of you says, "I am a follower of Paul," and another says, "I follow Apollos," aren't you acting just like people of the world?
>
> After all, who is Apollos? Who is Paul? We are only God's

> servants through whom you believed the Good News. Each of us did the work the Lord gave us. I planted the seed in your hearts, and Apollos watered it, but it was God who made it grow. . . . For no one can lay any foundation other than the one we already have—Jesus Christ. (1 Cor. 3:4–6, 11)

Our human tendency is to follow or believe in others before God Himself. But if we are serious about experiencing freedom in all its fullness, we need to be willing to ask a hard and honest question.

Who will we trust to work out the miracles and everyday moments in our lives?

The Maker, the made, or me?

The Source Determines the Course

As daughters of God, we have only two sources of empowerment we can choose from. We understand that we are given authority from someone else, usually from a higher power over us or a person with a higher standing. Or we choose to give ourselves the power, which means we believe we can create the power we need from within.

If we are living from source number two, *we are the responsible party.* We will carry the load that comes from maintaining control, even if it drains us dry. Responsibility is no small thing. Before we decide which source of empowerment to choose, we have to be willing to deal with the consequences of results resting on us. When things go wrong, we will be the one others and ourselves blame. This path inevitably leads to shame, which means it's the course Satan wants us to take.

However, when we operate from source number one, we'll view life through a liberating lens, and any present shame may sting but won't last. Dr. Tony Evans has a saying: "God is the source. Everything else is a resource."[1] The apostle Paul summarized this truth by saying, "For from him and through him and to him are all things" (Rom. 11:36 ESV). We could have all the resources in the world to help us get the job done effectively, including our own personality and gifts from God. But without a constant source empowering us, these resources will dry up and we will eventually burn out.

Jesus doesn't want this for us. He wants to transition our spirits from residing in a parched land to thriving in the promised land—a place where our power comes from the living water He provides.

So we need to make a choice. We've been invited to become gospel-centered women, not women centered around self. Our faith cannot be shaken when Christ is our foundation because overcoming depends on what God has done on our behalf. This is complete foolishness to the world. They cannot grasp how trusting in God can bring confidence, since we lose a sense of control.

But believing we are in control does not mean we are sovereign. We may think we need to maintain control in order to make things happen, but no human can hold on long enough to last a lifetime. Eventually, our sore hands will need to loosen their grip.

What's So Bad About Believing in Yourself?

Can we pause here for a second? It's really important I clarify myself so you don't think I'm saying something I'm not. When I say we shouldn't believe in ourselves, I'm not saying we can't be proud of what we've done or give ourselves a well-deserved pat on the back. *We can be proud without being prideful.* I tell my boys I'm proud of them. I let them know I see the hard work they put into making things happen, as does God. He is proud of His kids like we are proud of our own.

However, in the words of Paul, we can plant, plow, and sow, but God is the One who makes it grow. The Bible tells us there's a reward for working together with Christ, and that reward will present itself as a ripe harvest. Even if the harvest isn't what we expected or it looks different than we hoped, we can rejoice when blessings, dreams, and God's plans come to pass.

But many followers cross a critical line.

The Bible contains numerous stories of people doing well trusting God, but then they started placing their faith in their own performance rather than their Father's. David, Samson, Solomon, Moses, Sarah, and Abraham, just to name a few, all let their flesh put *self* as the cornerstone of their confidence instead of the Creator. I could easily add myself to the list of sisters and brothers who have attempted to take over God's job. Being a human called to holiness is *hard*. That's why we need Jesus.

Culture will continue to be the cheerleader for taking matters into our own hands because proclaiming belief in ourselves resonates with society's (and Satan's) agenda. Meanwhile, God is the One who is pushed out of the picture instead of the One we push into.

Our walks as Christ-empowered women can be summarized as such: *we need to be diligent and dependent on God at the same time.* We can try our hardest and also trust God's handiwork. This mindset will help us stay in balance as we live out what we believe.

Is Knowledge Really Power?

Sir Francis Bacon once said, "Knowledge is power."[2] Even though this statement may have good motives behind it, knowledge by itself lacks the transformative punch. God's Word makes it clear that raw knowledge does not produce saving belief. James, the earthly brother of Jesus, wrote to the early Jewish believers saying, "You say you have faith, for you believe that there is one God. Good for you! Even the demons believe this, and they tremble in terror" (James 2:19). I remember reading this for the first time and thinking, "Wait, this has to be a typo. Demons believe in God too? How is my belief different from theirs?" Praise God, the difference is night and day.

Knowledge takes root in the *head*. Belief takes root in the *heart*.

We can know something is true and choose not to trust it. Our enemy and his demons know about God. They recognize Christ's authority, but they rebel instead of repenting. They sin instead of submitting. They don't trust God, even though God is the standard for all truth.

Knowledge is only powerful if belief backs it. Instead of only knowing about God, we need to know Him personally and rely on Him for everything, ranging from salvation to sanctification. When we believe in the character and capability of God, our actions will inevitably follow. As the title of this book proclaims: we believe HE can, so we step out in faith and do!

But sometimes our actions get lost in translation. James encountered a problem in early believers that still echoes within our church walls. Because of intense persecution, early believers had a hard time backing their beliefs with their behaviors.

The main message in the book of James is that faith needs to be fleshed out or it's dead. This is something I'm very familiar with. For the first fifteen years of my walk with God, my faith was flatlined. I'd rather clothe myself in popularity than Christ. Being liked was more important than being His. But then the emptiness inside my soul grew. No matter how many troubled relationships I was in, no matter how many drinks I downed at the bar, no matter how high the grade I received, nothing could make me believe I was worth being loved. Only Jesus could show me that by believing in Him I also had the opportunity to believe I was valuable as God's child. Beloved. Chosen. Important. Called.

Believing in God's opinion about His children helps us transition from having an unsteady identity to an unbreakable one. As we get to know God more, we fall more in love with Him. And as we spend more time with Him, we start to imitate Him, which makes us look different from those who do not have a relationship with Christ.

Possessing knowledge about Jesus is not the same as truly knowing Jesus and being changed by His personhood. This tangible transformation testifies to a faith that's truly alive.

When Belief Gets Misused . . .

Consider highlighting these next two sentences. *We are not believers in the power of our actions. We are believers in the power of our God.*

Sometimes the idea of belief gets misused because we make it our fault if something we are trusting God for doesn't come to fruition. Maybe you've been told you don't have "enough faith," insinuating that if something you're trusting God for doesn't happen as you expected, you're somehow to blame. Let's challenge this line of thinking.

Wouldn't this mindset be focused on self-dependence again, placing pressure on us to produce the right amount of faith needed to yield the miracle or make God's hand move? Isn't this a different version of salvation through works, except this time we are working toward extravagant faith?

The last time I looked, God was in charge of what unfolds.

Think about Jesus' disciples. These men walked, talked, slept, and broke bread with the Messiah. They saw daily wonders and witnessed the Word of the Lord change lives, including their own. Yet they doubted. They struggled in trusting Christ with their fears, even though they experienced His physical presence.

I think this may be why Jesus said to "doubting" Thomas after His resurrection, "You believe because you have seen me. Blessed are those who believe without seeing me" (John 20:29). It's far easier to believe what we see with our own eyes. But believing in Christ without touching His scarred hands, that is a choice that deems us blessed.

Ephesians 2:8–9 says, "For by grace you have been saved through faith. And this is not your own doing; it is the gift of God, not a result of works, so that no one may boast" (ESV). Ultimately, faith is a gift from God that benefits our sanctification—our ongoing growth in Christ—not just our salvation. We don't possess the ability to believe, or have faith, without the softening work of the Holy Spirit in our hearts. God draws us to Himself. He gives us the spiritual gift of faith so we can choose to believe truth and obey our King. Everything starts and ends with God, including our belief.

I was reading to my boys before bed the other night, and we were enjoying *Thoughts to Make Your Heart Sing* by Sally Lloyd-Jones. The reading was based off an important verse in Mark, "I do believe, but help me overcome my unbelief!" (Mark 9:24). Children's books can be the most profound. The author wrote, "Our strong God is the one who rescues us—not our strong faith. Because faith isn't just you holding on to God. It's God holding on to you."[3] When Jesus called His disciples, He didn't require perfect faith to follow Him. He asked for willing people who were learning to believe because God's heart had taken hold of theirs.

Let's dive a little deeper here. When Jesus said to His disciples, "O ye of little faith," what did He mean? It's likely He was not referring to the quantity but the quality of their faith, mainly their lack of faith in Him despite what they'd seen Him accomplish. This leads to an important realization.

God cares more about *surrendered* faith than the size of our faith. Instead of calling us to believe bigger, perhaps we are created to believe in the bigness of our God.

The fact is, Jesus healed and performed miracles for those who believed and those who didn't. Not everyone who experienced a miracle decided to follow Him. God is uncannily gracious like that. Even after people chose to become His disciples, Jesus did not ask them to have enormous faith because bigger is not always better in the kingdom of God. What really matters in our relationship with Christ is our daily faithfulness to Him and our belief in what He is capable of doing. Jesus didn't say to muster up enough faith. Instead, He referenced the mustard seed, one of the smallest seeds known in that point of history.

"If you had *faith even as small as a mustard seed*, you could say to this mountain, 'Move from here to there,' and it would move. Nothing would be impossible" (Matt. 17:20). It's not about gathering large amounts of faith; it's about the presence of the seed and its ability to impact our trust in God as He moves. Small faith can shift mountains. The tiniest amount of belief is enough for God to do what *He* wills.

Another aspect that is overlooked when people are told they don't have enough faith is the reality of God's sovereignty. I've struggled with chronic pain, which has even landed me in the hospital. I asked for prayer and received tons of support when lying in that cold hospital bed. But there were moments when I wondered what I'd done wrong to not receive the healing God has promised. God didn't put those thoughts there; well-intentioned people in my life did. They asked me if I had sin, unforgiveness, unresolved trauma, or lies I was believing about my identity in Christ. They implied that if these things existed, then that's why I wasn't being healed.

Can trauma and our belief systems affect our bodies? Absolutely. Can healing happen once God has addressed those deep wounds? Definitely. Can we even be challenged to believe God can do the miraculous? Of course! But putting a one-size-faith-fits-all expectation on those who are experiencing unwanted symptoms or other kinds of personal challenges can generate an atmosphere of shame, especially if they are following through with advice that's been given to them. Personally, I began to think *not* receiving a miracle was my fault. I wondered whether my mustard seed of faith was as good as others.' Maybe I wasn't loved as much as they were?

This is a dangerous line of thinking because it gives way to the enemy's voice. The second we begin to question the love of our Father, we need to check our thoughts because they aren't coming from heaven.

They're coming from hell. Satan wants to pile shame on top of our pain, hoping we turn away from God by doubting His ability or care.

Saying someone is not healed or delivered because of their lack of faith is a judgment I am not comfortable making because I am not the all-knowing God. I've seen God work the miraculous and do the impossible. I believe He can do it. But I also believe He is loving and faithful to His followers no matter what happens on this side of heaven.

Here's a truth I pray will bring you as much freedom as it has me: *We cannot earn God's healing.*

Just like we can't earn God's love, we can't prove to God why we deserve healing. God's heart is already turned toward healing His kids and He will do it—it's just a matter of when.

Healing does come at a cost, but it isn't a price *we* had to pay. Jesus paid for our restoration through His death, which means any type of healing we may experience on earth—whether it's the healing gift of salvation, relational healing, physical healing, or others—occurs because of Christ's sacrifice, not our striving. This is the backdrop we need when reading stories like Job's.

Job is often an unsettling narrative for various reasons. He lost everything—his family, health, possessions, security. This wasn't done because he was sinning but because he was righteous. God allowed Job to be shaken by suffering because "there is none like him on the earth, a blameless and upright man, who fears God and turns away from evil" (Job 1:8 ESV). These are words from the mouth of God. Job did nothing to merit the suffering he endured.

And yet, Job's response to loss was one God approves of and understands. Throughout the book, God's beloved servant rode waves of grief, doubt, and conviction. He was honest with God. He was emotional and upset. But he continued to turn his face toward the Lord, even in the middle of the most gut-wrenching suffering a human can bear. Job's faith was purified and perfected because of the pain.

What can we say to this? Well, Job's three friends tried to say a lot. They wanted to reason with Job and find a *why* for his suffering. But they actually ended up misunderstanding and misusing truth regarding hardship. God was allowing Satan to mess with Job not because of Job's sin. He used Job's suffering in order to make him more like the coming Savior.

Christ's sole mission was to bring about His Father's will above all else. And what is God's ultimate will? To save the relationship between humanity and Himself, no matter what it takes. Jesus' prayer to avoid death in the final hours of His life was not passed over because He lacked belief. It was answered differently because God saw the bigger plan of redemption at hand. God's sovereignty will always reign.

Blessed Is She Who Believes . . .

I'd love to finish the story about our dog.

On the morning of the third day my oldest son woke me up out of a quasi sleep very early. He grabbed my hand and said, "Mom, the sky is orange but look! There's a rainbow." I stumbled my way to the window and saw the most unique sky I have ever seen. Orange clouds lingered in the air above the houses, and an entire rainbow arched across the sky, covering the length of the cornfields where our Callie went missing. As the tears began to well up, I remembered how the Lord keeps His promises and I knew He would remain faithful to our family. In the sacredness of that moment, my broken heart decided once again to believe.

I got in the car and searched with my boy and our other dog, Jack. We looked around for two hours with no sight of Callie. I came back home confused. I thought the rainbow was a sign from God that I would find her then and there. Instead, I returned feeling like I was torturing myself by continuing to look for her.

Then it started to rain—and desperation set in.

I told the kids to get their shoes and coats on because we were going to ask the nearby farmers if we could search their barns. Then my mom called my husband. She had a nudge from God to go look for Callie one more time out by the cornfield where she initially went missing. When she arrived on the scene, she was shocked. There was Callie, sitting near the road in the cornfield behind our street, the exact area the rainbow arched over that morning! Perhaps God in His kindness was showing us where He would lead our girl home. My mom told my husband, Madison, to head to the field and he sprinted out the door.

Meanwhile, Callie was still in survival mode. Even though she knew my husband, she darted from him and ran onto our street. Madison called me in the pouring rain. I could barely hear him say "Get outside on the porch! Callie is coming!" I sprinted out front, hoping and holding my breath.

As I looked across the street, my heart jumped. There she was! Standing still, frozen in fright. I'm sure she smelled her family and recognized where she was, but she was too scared. She looked at us cautiously while I got down on my knees and gently called her name.

Dear God, please don't let her run again, I prayed silently.

She stared. She listened. She took a few steps in our direction before starting to run in between our house and our neighbor's.

Jesus, no! I continued calling her name.

At the last second, she made a sharp turn toward us, running right into my arms. I gripped my girl tightly and helped her get inside as the tears poured uncontrollably down my face. Our family has never cried so hard in our lives. God had reunited us! He was the One who called our Callie home.

What a faithful King we serve. What a capable God we have. He makes the impossible possible and the miraculous a reality. So much so that our spirits can sing *only God.*

We don't need to have faith in anyone else when we have a Father who loves us and fights for us. We don't need to believe in ourselves if our God is eternally on our side. He is for us, with us, and in us.

We can trust His forever faithfulness.

Let's finish with one of my favorite verses on belief. It applies to Mary after she found out she was going to carry the Savior of the world in her womb. Her reaction to God's promises brought her praise from Elizabeth, her cousin. Elizabeth exclaimed, "And *blessed is she who believed* that there would be a fulfillment of what was spoken to her from the Lord" (Luke 1:45 ESV). Even when others thought she was lying or crazy, Mary held on to God, knowing He was holding on to her. She didn't strive to accumulate more faith in God; she practiced surrendered faith. After the angel told Mary what was to come, she responded by saying, "I am the Lord's servant. May everything you have said about me come true" (Luke 1:38).

Oh, that we'd all have a heart like Mary.

Blessed is she who believes in her God.

Be blessed, my friend.

Stories from Sisters Who Believed HE Could

JODI'S STORY:

"God, help me today. I don't have the strength." Alone in my king-sized bed, these words turned into my prayer. With my pen in hand, my journal became my safe haven to express to God all the pain and hurt as I struggled to keep my head above water from the waves of grief from my divorce.

There were so many emotions: the intense sadness that weighed heavily on my heart because my kids would grow up in a divorced home, the deep rejection and brokenness I felt from the one who promised to love me forever, and the great shame that haunted my mind as I thought about my failed marriage. These overwhelming feelings were like a weight on my body, making it hard to do simple things like get out of bed and face the day. On top of it all, I was trying to comfort my hurting children while dealing with the greatest heartbreak of my life. It's no wonder I was tired and exhausted.

With tears rolling down my face, I cried out to God, asking for His help. My own strength wasn't enough to weather this storm. I needed to turn to the One who could calm the raging emotions in my heart and mind.

The world tries to tell us if we believe enough in ourselves, we can conquer anything. But I'd come to a crossroads in my pain where this wasn't true. I needed to depend on God's strength, comfort, and love to get through the grief. Learning total dependence on God was a beautiful gift in the middle of my brokenness, and God wants to do the same for us all! He desires to strengthen and comfort us in our unexpected storms. The real question is, Do we believe God is enough? (*Jodi R. from California*)

Chapter 5

~~SPEAK YOUR TRUTH~~

SHARE YOUR STORY, BUT SPEAK *THE* TRUTH

I didn't realize I experienced sexual assault until years after we broke up. I thought being in a relationship with a guy meant it was okay to go to the very edge of the line without physically sleeping with each other, even if in my spirit I didn't feel like it was right. I didn't want to be rejected or cast in a negative light.

So when my boyfriend at the time asked me to take another step toward sex, I decided losing my purity bit by bit was better than losing him. He wasn't mean or aggressive, just ongoing and persistent. I chose to not say *stop* even though I wanted to. Sometimes I tried to convince myself I was overreacting. Other times I stayed silent, which I found out later did not equal consent.[1]

Technically, I saved myself until marriage, but only by a hairline thread. I could claim the "true love waits" tune as my own, but felt buried in inner condemnation and self-hate. The gift of sex with my husband was tainted by my past, affecting the way I loved myself and my body. But God had already started to align my feelings and thoughts regarding what had happened with who I truly was in Him.

After beginning to walk with Jesus more closely in college, I chose to open up more and shared my experiences with close friends, which was a big step in my healing journey. They helped me realize I didn't need to say *yes* to sexual acts when I didn't want to or because the world portrayed these actions as normal in relationships. God wanted to protect me and pour His love into the wounded parts of my spirit hiding in the shadows of shame.

One day the Lord gave me a visual of how He really saw me. On a beautiful, sandy beach we were walking barefoot, laughing as the waves rolled gently against our feet. When I looked down at my clothes I saw I was wearing a flowing white linen dress with an intricate emerald necklace. My hair was wavy and long and flying gracefully in the wind. In a word, I felt *free.*

Years later, as my fiancé (now husband) and I were picking out a passage to read at our wedding, we landed on Isaiah 61:1–3. We met while doing missions work and felt that it would be the perfect fit for the life of ministry we wanted to lead as a couple and family. This passage also echoed the words of Jesus Himself when He announced the beginning of His earthly public ministry. Only recently have I seen the significance in the verses just beyond the beginning of our wedding passage—Scripture that eradicates the lies remaining from the aftermath of sin and pain. "I will greatly rejoice in the Lord; my soul shall exult in my God, for he has clothed me with the *garments of salvation*; he has *covered me with the robe of righteousness,* as a bridegroom decks himself like a priest with a beautiful headdress, and as a *bride adorns herself with her jewels*" (Isa. 61:10 ESV).

The Word of God confirmed the picture Jesus had given me—a pure bride, covered in white, with Christ's righteousness as her wardrobe. No stain or blemish on her garment because she has been rescued from disgrace and is redeemed by the blood of her Bridegroom. The truth of who we are as God's beloved is what allows our hearts and spirits to live in liberty.

Sharing our stories is a necessary ingredient in experiencing healing, because once we bring to light what happened in the darkness, whether it be sexual assault or any other sin that's been committed against or by us, we disarm the enemy's weapons of isolation and condemnation. But hear me when I say that sharing our stories is not *the* transforming agent in our healing. "So Jesus said to the Jews who had believed him, 'If you abide in my word, you are truly my disciples, and you will know the truth, and the truth will set you free'" (John 8:31–32 ESV).

Abiding in the Word and knowing the truth sets us free! It isn't *my* truth or any other person's truth that brings the freedom our souls crave. Yes, we can learn from others and gain wisdom from the experiences others have had, particularly when we've suffered through the same heartbreaking situations. But if we long to heal at the deepest level possible, we need to let *the* truth permeate through the lies, reaching within to the parts of us that are processing who we are to God, ourselves, and others.

The truth of the gospel rescued and healed me. And it can do the same for all God's daughters.

What Is Truth?

The question of what truth really is has been asked throughout the ages, but one scene in history stands out and is documented in Scripture.

Pontius Pilate was questioning Jesus before His crucifixion. The Jewish religious elite had finally gotten their way and were hoping to put Jesus to death through the workings of Rome's harsh governing system. The Pharisees couldn't handle Christ's existence any longer with His countercultural teachings and "unclean" methods of ministry among the people. Plus, this man had claimed to be the Son of God with the ability to forgive sins, heal the sick, and cast out demons. Christ's authority was threatening the perceived notion of their own.

It is here that we see this famous question asked by Pilate. After Pilate asked if Jesus was the King of the Jews,

> Jesus answered, "You say that I am a king. For this purpose I was born and for this purpose I have come into the world—*to bear witness to the truth.* Everyone who is of the truth listens to my voice." Pilate said to him, "*What is truth?*" After he had said this, he went back outside to the Jews and told them, "I find no guilt in him." (John 18:37–38 ESV)

Pilate tried releasing Jesus *at least* four times. This historically cruel and corrupt governor who was known for his brutality in carrying out orders was cautious in sentencing the "King of the Jews."[2] Why? What was so different about this seemingly harmless man?

The fact that Pilate was conflicted in the presence of Jesus shows the authority of Christ and His character, but more specifically, what happens when someone stands in the presence of absolute Truth.

After finding out that Jesus had supposedly called Himself the Son of God, the Bible says Pilate "was even more afraid" (John 19:8 ESV). Could he have seen a foreshadowing of the reversal of their roles, when Pilate would one day be placed on trial before God? Pilate's wife sent word to him while Pilate was in the process of passing judgment, asking her husband not to have anything to do with "that righteous man" because she was distressed by a dream she had about Jesus (Matt. 27:19 ESV). In response, Pilate visibly washed his hands before the crowd demanding Jesus' execution and said, "I am innocent of this man's blood. The responsibility is yours!" (Matt. 27:24).

In all these accounts, there's a spectrum of reactions to Christ. From

Pilate's wavering stance to the religious leaders' hardened hearts, when a person encounters Truth, a decision must be made. *Will we reject it, ignore it, fear it, or submit to Truth's voice?* While we as God's children aren't passing judgment on the King of kings, we do have the choice to react to the truths God reveals and speaks to our hearts. What is truth? Truth changes every aspect of our lives, which explains why we often do not receive it well.

Our culture has an interesting relationship with truth. People say they want it, but they also want truth that doesn't cause offense or inconvenience. Having a subjective definition of truth is much safer when society's opinions are what counts. This is a dangerous decision, however, when applied to walking out our faith. We may begin to fashion God into our desired form instead of letting God do the transforming.

J. I. Packer wrote, "A half-truth masquerading as the whole truth becomes a complete untruth."[3]

We can soak up half-truths all day, but they don't heal the eternal parts of our souls. We can share our stories and speak *our* truth until we are out of breath, but if we don't use the Bible as *the foundation* for truth, complete healing will come to a halt. The world and the enemy are full of partial truths that mask Christ as the Healer. Viewing any untruths in the light of God's Word will clearly illuminate their cracks.

Take the title of this book as a prime example.

By removing one letter from the sentence *She Believed ~~S~~HE Could, So She Did*, we go from being self-focused to God-focused. We are able to look at a saying that didn't sit quite right and realize the reason is that it's a half-truth. As we discussed earlier, strength is meant to be sourced in God, not our self-made grit. Diligence and hard work may be biblical, but doing it independently from our Creator will only result in frustration and burnout.

Half-truths like *speak your truth* end up leading women down a path that will ultimately make them crumble under a weight they were never meant to carry. It's not all relative. There is an objective and absolute reality. It isn't based on our ever-changing feelings, thoughts, and experiences, and it certainly isn't based on popular trends. Myths masquerading as facts will make women feel lost instead of liberated. But truth grounded in love will care for the soul the way it was meant to be mended.

Speaking *the* Truth in Love No Matter What

Take a few moments to look on social media and you will see it's a hot mess. People want others to know what they believe and why they can't possibly be wrong about their opinions. They want their voices heard, even if it means hurting others through unkind words. *Speaking your truth* has become the anthem of our days.

The idea of absolutes, of black-and-white answers with little room for gray, makes people feel uncomfortable and sometimes can be viewed as unloving. How can we say we know what's definite when so many opinions and perspectives fill our planet? Isn't it prideful to say you know the only way? Couldn't this mindset hurt relationships or your opportunities to talk to others about Christ?

In order to answer these questions, I have to ask another. When did speaking the truth imply comfortableness? Who said we had to avoid difficult conversations in order to be loving? Certainly not Jesus.

Right after the Lord tells His disciples to love one another, He says, "If the world hates you, remember that it hated me first. The world would love you as one of its own if you belonged to it, but you are no longer part of the world. I chose you to come out of the world, so it hates you" (John 15:18–19).

The world hates those who go against its grain. It won't favor those having difficult conversations with family and friends. Pushback will happen and it may be severe. In the Western world, the pushback we experience is less physical than the persecution felt in countries where following Christ is punishable by death.

But we are all called to mature into the mind and likeness of Jesus, and then share the truth with others. "Rather, speaking the truth in love, we are to grow up in every way into him who is the head, into Christ" (Eph. 4:15 ESV). In the previous verses Paul addressed believers who shouldn't be childish anymore, like those tossed back and forth between man-made philosophies or the false teachings of the age, which are appealing and cunning.

Rather, we are told to speak truth with love. The two go together. Love is our motivation. Truth is our foundation. Together they balance each other out in perfect harmony.

When we love someone and we know what will help them, is it loving to withhold our words because we don't want to offend them? Yes, we must rely on the Holy Spirit to guide us in knowing what and when to speak. But if we have access to the Healer and do not give people the chance to receive His restorative balm, is this done out of fear or love? This is a conversation Jesus and I have often, and He convicts me of choosing myself instead of what's beneficial for others. I can struggle with being rejected by others, but because I love them, I'd rather they reject me over rejecting God.

Love also does not mean accepting what everyone else says (including our pastors and leaders) as the gospel truth. There is only one gospel that unites us as believers, and we must make sure we are grounded in its fullness. Without truth, love would just be laissez-faire affections going with the ebb and flow of everyone's beliefs. This kind of love would be more concerned with placating than pastoring.

It can be tempting in our churches to focus on powerful testimonies and meaningful stories, but when we shift away from applying Scripture to the stories we tell, we end up giving watered-down truths, or worse yet, a watered-down gospel. Partially watering a soul will still leave the soil dry. We need the entirety of God's unwavering narrative and character, not just snippets that fit our faith or worldviews, in order to quench a person's thirst for truth.

When believers only welcome versions of Christ that fit their lifestyle and wants, they are actually allowing their half-truths to make a half-Christ.

They'll load up on a loving, gracious Jesus. They'll take the Savior who's a friend. But truth-speaking, take-a-stand-on-the-Word-even-if-the-world-hates-you Jesus gets left on the shelf. Standing up for the real gospel was never easy for the disciples, and it won't be easy for us. Comfort was never promised for a life made to stand out.

Why We Need Truth

We all have experiences that need to be validated and understood. When someone shares their story from their perspective and discloses what they're feeling, it shouldn't be dismissed. This is a huge part of showing compassion, listening, and giving love. But sharing your story does not downplay the existence of absolute Truth. Both can coexist at the same time. However, in order to experience the Lord's healing, our beliefs need to be held next to the inspired Word of God. You can share your story but also cling to what's true.

Let's say you have a neighbor. She's great, except anytime you walk outside during the day, she tells you it's night. You look up, you feel the sun, you see the light. But she is convinced it's dark. The world would try to convince you that both of you are entitled to your own "truth"—that one person's reality isn't always right. Meanwhile, nature literally shows us how absolutes exist. Nighttime earth faces away from the sun, daytime earth faces toward the sun. It's either day or night in your neighborhood because they can't happen at the same time.

To say there are no absolute truths is to deny how our physical world works. The Bible tells us how the seen points to what is unseen. If absolute truths exist in the physical world, they exist in the spiritual even more.

Ironically, declaring truth as something that can encompass everyone's beliefs will only end up making nothing true at all. This would create a world that is confused and hurting and does not know where to look for direction. Sounds familiar, right?

Again, there is room for subjective realities in our lives because of our different experiences, circumstances, and pasts, but we need to submit our processing to Jesus—who calls Himself *the* way, *the* truth, and *the* life. We shouldn't be afraid to point out the undercurrent of truth in all we do and see. Even those who don't realize it yet need a reliable foundation to walk on. We need the steady Rock that won't break.

Okay, I didn't want to share this story, but I will, even though it's embarrassing. I hate buying shorts. I don't know whose body they use to model shorts, but it definitely isn't mine. Well, I went shopping at Walmart last summer and to my shock they had super cute navy blue shorts that looked good on me and didn't break the bank. Walmart for the win. Or so I thought.

The next day I put on my cute new shorts and drove my boys to day camp. I got out of the car and talked to their counselor as other parents dropped off their kids. Then I went to the gas station and filled up the car and completed another errand before heading over to my mom's house to say hi. When I arrived at her house I gave her a hug, told her about my Walmart win, and proceeded to sit down until Mom pointed something out to me.

"Do you know there's a hole in the back of your shorts?"

"What?!" Well, no, Mother, I did not. In fact, I was feeling quite sassy in my shorts as I ran *all around town* that morning. From my point of view, everything seemed fine. But in reality, I had a three-inch rip down the center seam line of my rear. Bless it, Jesus.

Thank God for my mom who wasn't afraid to tell me the truth. I can only imagine how many innocent bystanders would have been forced to see what they didn't want to see. I'm grateful for those who speak up and say what is true, even if it will make others feel uncomfortable or upset. As long as it is done in love and is led by the Holy Spirit, we can be glad others are bold enough to tell *the* truth versus the half-truth people want to hear. We can ask God to make us those kind of truth tellers as well.

The Path Toward Real Healing

Searching for spiritual and emotional healing can be tricky. We can experience *temporary* healing through man-made programs and ideas, but *total* healing can only come through Jesus Christ. If we pile on Band-Aids to cover a serious wound but don't clean out the bacteria, an infection can fester beneath the surface. Unfortunately, I know this from a physical, mental, and emotional standpoint.

When I first became a mama, our birth experience was nothing like we expected. We wanted to be prepared and brought our eighteen-page birth plan to the hospital, to which the nurses smiled (and I'm sure thought "bless your heart"). They didn't give it a second glance.

After twenty-seven hours of intense labor and three hours of pushing, our baby boy was still wedged inside of me and both of our vitals started to drop. The next thing I knew, I was being rolled off to an emergency C-section and within half an hour we had our son in our hands. But recovery for me did not go smoothly.

My incision site became infected, and I had to be reopened and packed with gauze two times a day until my large cut closed. It was extremely painful, but crucial for repairing my body the way it needed. Little by little, from the inside out, with care and precision, my cut closed and the infection ceased. Band-Aids wouldn't do for this kind of deep wound. Now my scar tells the story of powerful healing done right.

Jesus wants to remove anything that threatens to infect our hearts, including lies and unbiblical beliefs. He doesn't want His daughters relying on half-truths that will leave their souls aching. God wants our whole being healed and free, where blame is banished and fear is expelled. Christ has more for us, more than this world and its inferior forms of empowerment and healing can offer.

Besides rooting our identity in God's love and reacquainting ourselves with the realities of God's Word, healing can also be found within community. When we share our brokenness with others, the beauty of recognition and restoration is on the other side. Finding those we trust, who will tend to our wounded parts and carry us back to Jesus, is as necessary as air. Christ-centered fellowship fosters freedom, as fellow sisters say *I've been there too.*

Sharing leads to caring, which then can help us conquer.

The enemy of our souls wants women to remain blind to the healing they could have. Many times, we can't see what's wrong unless a mirror is held in front of us, and even then, we may miss inner injuries because we can't see them. But having other women in our lives who know us and have suffered through similar situations brings a life-giving power that encourages us to take the next steps toward the treatment we need, especially when we can't see clearly or we don't feel like we have the strength to move on. God uses other people as a physical expression of His friendship and His guidance going forward. When we don't have the faith, God gives us sisters who will have faith for us.

Healing is done hand in hand.

Scripture says we overcome the enemy by the blood of the Lamb and the word of our testimony (Rev. 12:11). We need to share our stories not just because it helps us remember the faithfulness of God but because it stops Satan's schemes. Instead of allowing the enemy to sequester us into pockets of shame, we refuse to stay silent and share our stories for the benefit of our spirits and others. We open our mouths and speak God's promises over our past, present, and future. Meanwhile, we are communally drawn closer to Christ. We defeat the devil and declare the truths of the gospel each time we share our story and speak *the* truth.

And what is the truth for you, dear reader?

No matter what's been done to you, no matter what's been said, no one can take away the truth about who you are to Jesus. He's adorned you with radiant righteousness and calls you part of the church, His spotless bride. The scars He has on His body testify to the depths of His love. You cannot measure the grace He pours out over your life or the healing He wants for your heart. Let His precious truth wash over your spirit in the most tender places today.

Stories from Sisters Who Believed HE Could

AMY'S STORY:

Learning the difference between God's truth and the world's truth has been a journey for me. Growing up, I lived in eighteen different homes, and at the age of eleven, I was sexually exploited. My unaddressed pain led me to believe many lies about who I was and whether God really loved me. The world's lies, which were masked as truth, kept me isolated from God and the life-giving community I desperately needed.

In God's great faithfulness, He pursued me and met me where I was. He taught me the value of spending time with Him and His promises for my life. Trauma has a way of distorting all that's good and true, but God has a way of restoring and rebuilding beautiful back into the lives of His daughters.

After a life-changing trip to Africa, I founded a nonprofit that empowers the rescue and restoration of exploited women and children. Ten years later, more than a thousand lives have been miraculously changed.

Friend, your history may have marked you, but it is not authorized to label you. It doesn't matter what other people have called you, and it doesn't even matter what you called yourself. There's only one who has the right and authority to tell you who you are—God. His truth is the only truth that matters!

So what can we say to ourselves when we feel overwhelmed by life or heartache from our past? Here are three truths worth remembering:

1. Remember *who God is.*
2. Remember *who you are in Christ.*
3. Remember, *God's truth is greater than your own.*

May we experience the freedom that comes from speaking *God's truth* over every aspect of our lives through the Word of God. He is always with us. He hears us when we cry out to Him. And He has promised never to leave. (*Amy K. from Ohio*)

Chapter 6

~~FOLLOW YOUR HEART~~
FOLLOW YOUR KING

For the majority of my life I felt like my existence as a person was too much. I was too needy. Too soft. Too sensitive. Too much for anyone to deal with. Resentment toward God began to fester as I questioned why He created me with deep emotions and longings. Based off a few relationships, I assumed others didn't want to know who I really was. Maybe if they knew me at the depth of my core, they'd shake their heads and walk away. Eventually, I wondered if anyone could ever handle my heart. It didn't seem likely.

"You're being too *sensitive*, Becky."

This phrase echoed throughout my childhood and early adult years. Family. Friends. Boyfriends. When used by them, the word *sensitive* implied an imperfection. It hinted at something I should alter or some sin that required repentance. Eventually I started to feel bad for feeling. I associated sensitivity with shame and emotions with instability.

And so, because I didn't want to face the familiar sting of rejection, I began to hide my real self, choosing to fade away—until the Father stepped in.

Do these sentiments sound familiar to you? Has the word *sensitive* been used as a means of correcting what's wrong instead of complimenting what's right? If so, I've got some fascinating and freeing news. *We are not the only ones.*

In her book *The Highly Sensitive Person*, Elain Aron talks about many benefits of being someone who feels deeply, along with other character traits. According to Aron, around 20 percent of the population can be categorized as highly sensitive people.[1] That's one out of every five people we meet! Sensitivity is knit into people's DNA, something intentionally shaped by our Creator. God didn't fashion feelings by mistake; He formed them for His purpose. It took me decades to understand that the spectrum of emotions is seen in Scripture. Just because some people don't know how to appreciate them, it doesn't mean emotions are not beneficial.

Following the life of Jesus has helped me see how deep feelers should be viewed as a gift, not a grievance. Sensitivity is a needed trait for connecting with God and others. It also helps with building His diverse kingdom. Even if we are not highly sensitive people, God still made humans to have healthy and active emotions. God is the originator of feelings, and because we are made in His image, we are made to reflect *His* feelings as well. Note the emphasis on our *Creator's* heart because culture wants to put your heart above His.

Letting God Handle and Hold Our Hearts

Emotions are important. All too often, feelings can be disregarded in the pursuit of holiness when, in reality, we can take our feelings into the presence of the Holy One. God desires for us to be women who take our hearts seriously as we hand them over to Him.

So, let's kill one lie immediately: you will never be too much for Jesus.

It's okay if you need to stop and say that out loud right now. I am continuing to internalize it too.

No emotion takes God by surprise or overwhelms Him to the point where He will walk away. God can handle our fullest selves with feelings pouring over the brim. He is the only One who is capable of carrying our complicated hearts, and it's something He *wants* to do.

This was such a freeing fact for me to accept, especially as someone who's wrestled with tying emotions to the truth. While reading Psalm 138 the other day, I noted that David (a fellow deep feeler) penned words that resonated with this struggle. He wrote, "The LORD will fulfill his purpose for me; your steadfast love, O LORD, endures forever. Do not forsake the work of your hands" (Ps. 138:8 ESV). We can see David's battle to believe God's promise, even though he is trying to hold on to truth! With one breath he proclaims God's faithfulness, and with the next he pleads for God to not forsake His work in his life. The emotional struggle is there in one sentence.

In Ellie Holcomb's book *Fighting Words*, she talks about the importance of holding both honesty and remembrance in our hands when we approach God in prayer. She wrote, "David has shown me that prayer makes room for both *remembrance* (declaring what is true) and *honesty* (declaring how we are actually feeling about that truth in the moment)."[2] It's beautiful to know that God doesn't want us to hold our feelings back from Him. He wants our honest, broken, pleading selves because He intends to ground our feelings in what's steadfast and true—in Himself.

When Jesus walked the earth, He didn't downplay the array of feelings happening in humanity's hearts. He understood that emotions are powerful, because He felt every type of emotion we can feel as a human and still was without sin. The Son always brought His feelings back to the Father. When we wonder how to process what is going on in our hearts with God, Christ is our model. He shows us how aligning our emotions with the Spirit and Scripture is the way to experience an abundant, transformative life.

According to Proverbs, our hearts are considered a central player in our walk with God. "Guard your heart above all else, for it determines the course of your life" (Prov. 4:23). *Above all else* . . . those are not light words. The ESV translation of this verse says "springs of life" flow from the heart. Can you picture it? Pure, clear water bubbling out, creating a steady flow that moves throughout the surrounding area, affecting the fruitfulness of the environment. Our hearts are meant to produce life-giving fruit when we are connected to God, and, in turn, this affects all aspects of our personhood.

That's why the emotions we feel in our hearts need to be guarded and tended to as a top priority. How we engage with our hearts will determine the path of our actions. But God doesn't expect us to know how to lead our own hearts. He gives us the ability to submit everything to Him, but not because His goal is to control us. God is sovereign, and He could have controlled us from the beginning, but He gave us choice instead. He wants our love but doesn't force us to love Him. He wants our obedience, but gives us the option . . . and the consequences. God wants to have a real relationship with us.

Our kind Creator desires to hold our hearts so close that our heartbeats will begin to coincide with His. God calls us to guard our hearts in order to grow them into a replica of Christ's.

Following Our Hearts Versus Guarding Our Hearts

I know what it's like to resent my feelings, but I've also struggled with allowing my feelings to lead my decisions and behaviors. It's a delicate dance to master—letting your heart feel but also letting God do the leading. The world hates God's way of leading because the road to life is too narrow. In fact, culture preaches against the biblical balance God wants for our lives.

Society will tell you following your heart means relying on your feelings as the compass for your choices. Happiness becomes the basis for whether we are thriving or not. We'll talk more about happiness in a minute. But let me tell you, as a married human, if my husband and I gauged the depth of our love solely on the happy pitter-patter feelings in our hearts, we would have broken up years ago. We would have followed our hearts to perceivably "greener pastures" because happiness determines whether we should stay in the relationship, right?

Except marriage isn't just any relationship. It's a covenant. It's a commitment to stay with each other through thick and thin, in sickness and health, for richer or poorer, till death do us part. It would really benefit couples if we added "in happiness or sorrows" to the marriage vows because we need a more realistic view of the messiness in marriage, not just wedded bliss.

Flourishing marriages are not built upon happiness; they are founded on unconditional love. Most conditions, including the ever-changing condition of our hearts, should not be the basis for separation. Many conditions in our marriage have caused stress and pain, including secret sin, special-needs parenting, financial trouble, health emergencies, differing beliefs, and more. But by the grace of Jesus, we have chosen to remain committed to each other.

The Bible does give cause for leaving a married relationship (various forms of abuse and adultery), but the world gives couples complete freedom to end things when enamored feelings wane. This has never been God's style.

The Lord chose to love us, to enter into a covenant relationship with us, not because it would make Him happy. He chose to love us because He is the definition of love, and He wanted to restore our disconnected relationship, which was the result of our sin. The death of Jesus on the cross was worth it to God because His longing to be with us was greater than the sacrifice it would take to make reconciliation happen. We became a desire of His heart. Christ pursues His bride, and as the book of Hosea in the Bible portrays, even when she is unfaithful to Him, He woos her with His love.

All of this to say, when imitating the way of Jesus, our emotions should not get the final say in our decisions. Our feelings need to be seasoned with the Spirit and our hearts need to be guarded, not followed. Even if culture tries to lure you into buying the lie, remember, our hearts cannot always be trusted. They don't always tell the whole or the logical or the God-centered story.

The book of Jeremiah says, "The human heart is the most deceitful of all things, and desperately wicked. Who really knows how bad it is?" (Jer. 17:9). Umm, ouch. "Deceitful" is another way of saying our hearts can begin to turn on us. According to this verse, the level of deception can get pretty bad if God is not in the mix. It's tricky because while we can see when someone else shouldn't be trusted, it's much more difficult for us to tell when we can't trust ourselves.

Feelings are influential. They can filter reality, but they cannot be trusted to serve as the basis for truth.

Know Whom You're Following

I've learned my lesson in highway traffic jams. I used to be a serial lane shifter. Now when I find myself in the slow lane, I usually stay there for a bit. In the past I would see which lane was moving fastest and then zoom over to catch up on time. The only problem is that everyone had the same idea so they would move too, and soon the faster lane would become the slow lane and the probability of pileups would rise. Following the crowd does not guarantee success.

I have always loved going to Disney World, but I cannot tell you how many times we've gotten in line for nothing in the theme parks. Literally, there was nothing at the end of the line. But people saw a line form and they assumed others knew what they were doing. We all gathered our sweaty (and often hangry) families, followed suit, and stood in line for nothingness. Both these examples point toward the importance of knowing and trusting whom you're following. If we are willing to follow strangers, how much more should we be invested in following our Savior?

Often society encourages us to deem ourselves the leader of our own lives because obviously, we should know what we really need. Our gut knows what's best. Our instincts won't lie. Our hearts know how to make us happy because, as the saying goes, "the heart wants what it wants" and there's just no stopping it. If King David wasn't in the presence of Jesus right now, I'm sure he would be rolling over in his grave to see believers living by this unbiblical advice.

David, who is termed *a man after God's own heart,* knew a few things about following your heart to the point of deception and destruction. He wanted Bathsheba, his friend's wife. He knew he shouldn't do it. He knew it wasn't right. Yet he followed his heart, leaving adultery and murder in the wake of his desire-driven decision. He went down a path he never thought he'd take and sent his friend to the front lines of battle in order to kill him and cover up a scandalous pregnancy. It worked. But it didn't fool God. The truth did come to the surface, along with some serious consequences for the sins he committed. Not the best argument out there for following your heart.

The message of self-empowerment says it's our job to satisfy our souls, not our Savior's. We have the right to do whatever it takes to make ourselves happy. Meanwhile, we ebb and flow throughout our days, following the delicate dance of our desires like David. But what if God's definition of happiness is not in line with ours? What if happiness is not the ultimate goal but merely a by-product of something even greater?

Does God Want Us to Be Happy?

Wouldn't a kind God want His children to be happy?

The answer is yes and no.

Of course, like any good parent, God isn't sitting up in heaven hoping His kids are miserable. When we go through heartbreak, His heart breaks with ours. He comforts us and makes Himself known in ways only grief and hardship can cultivate. But happiness is not the goal of a Christian life. Holiness and wholeness in Christ is.

Much of the Western world has been spared from the daily reality of persecuted disciples around the globe. Believers are being oppressed, discriminated against, and even killed for their faith in God. They face suffering, hardship, and pain on different levels than most of us ever will. And yet they choose to remain faithful to Jesus. *Why?*

They realize the power of the gospel does not promote one's happiness, but one's wholehearted devotion to a loving God. Jesus never promised His followers they would be happy. He promised they would see *joy* in tribulation, *contentment* in all circumstances, *peace* that surpasses understanding, and *love* in the midst of hate. These are the true markings of a believer in Christ. Not that they are following the desires of their own heart, but that they are following the ways of heaven.

Since the beginning, the enemy has influenced culture (and the church) to prioritize having a happy heart over a holy heart. The truth is, following God does not mean our lives will resemble some sort of fairy tale where happiness and pain-free living abound. Instead, following Jesus looks like laying our longings in His hands and trusting Him as He transforms our requests. There's a huge difference between following our hearts and following where God leads.

A beautiful transaction takes place when we give God our entire self, including our longings. Little by little, He begins to align our will with His. He replaces our desires with His dreams. With every act of relinquishment, we begin to see that our hearts beat simultaneously together.

We want what He wants.

We love what He loves.

We pursue what He pursues.

This perspective shift places the popular verse in Psalm 37 in the correct light. "Delight yourself in the LORD, and he will give you the desires of your heart" (Ps. 37:4 ESV). God isn't telling us to go after our pleasures. He's telling us to go after Him. To delight, to find joy, to smile at the thought of connecting with Jesus. This is the call on our hearts: to let ourselves be changed by the power of His character and care. In return, He will give us our desires because they are also His.

To set the record straight, God will never give us something that goes against His Word or will, so those misguided desires can be scratched off the list. God will also not serve as our personal genie who grants us whatever we please (and if He doesn't He's unkind or callous). We're not "living our best life now," although we are promised an abundant life with His principles and presence. God does rejoice with us when our earthly desires (which are in line with His heart) are fulfilled. But even if our longing still exists, that does not mean He does not see us or He has ceased being good.

For years, I've longed for a little girl. I've saved my childhood blanket, collected cute clothes, journaled countless prayers. When I went to school for discipleship and spiritual formation, I was excited to share this wisdom with my daughter one day. And God has blessed me with three amazing sons. I wouldn't change a thing. I want them. But I also would still love a little girl.

And so, I give this desire for a daughter to God. I trust Him with the yearning in my heart and believe He is wise and all-knowing and is working everything out for good. I can be honest with Him about the sadness that resides within my spirit, and I can remember His faithfulness to be enough for every aspect of my life. I can hold both realities in my hands at once and trust in His ability to bring me joy beyond my current situation. I can do all of this because I'm not led by my happiness. I'm led by sufficient grace.

Choosing a Devoted Heart over a Divided Heart

A. B. Simpson once wrote, "A divided heart loses both worlds."[3] It's a true statement for our souls. If we long to follow the way of the world, our hearts will never be completely satisfied. We will miss out on the delight of living fully for Christ and how that makes our hearts come alive! We can't be divided in our devotion to Jesus and expect our spirits to be all right. Division is uncomfortable. Even if we choose to go our own way, if we are God's child, His Spirit remains inside of ours, and we will not be "happy" without being connected to Him.

The heart may not know what it really wants, but it knows *who* it really needs. There's no doubt about it—our entire selves were created to be in communion with Christ.

God cares about us enough to give us a choice. We need to decide whom we will follow. *Our culture or our King.* Because we can't do both. We can't have one foot in Egypt and one foot in the promised land without feeling the widening rift. We need to devote our hearts solely to one or the other because lukewarm affection will result in apathy over awe.

In all my years of ministering to women, I have never met a Christian who said, "I wish God hadn't done X, Y, or Z with my heart . . . or healed my wounds . . . or heard my cries." We can trust God with our emotions as we process them all with Him. Jesus is worthy of receiving our feelings, friendship, and faith.

Following our King may not be the easiest choice to make, but it is the kindest thing we could ever do for our hearts.

Stories from Sisters Who Believed HE Could

MARNIE'S STORY:

"I can't handle you when you're like this." The words fell to my feet as the door closed. I stood alone in the room, stunned and confused.

I was carrying a lot, I remember. Stress seized my breath and anxiety locked my feet. Just before those words rocketed toward me, I'd followed my heart and offered a messy attempt at sharing the twisting I felt inside. In my muddled way, I was asking for help.

Instead, I found rejection.

A deep feeler, my confusion about how to navigate my heart stretches back decades. Tearstained pages of (terrible) poetry and hidden journals of (whiny) wonderings dated back to my teen years, bearing witness to my attempts at processing those tangled feelings.

If I tamped them down and held them quiet, I felt like an imposter. But following my heart and emotions created bigger messes. How does this "following your heart" thing work? Why doesn't acting on what I feel fix things?

After a string of broken and botched attempts to follow this heart of mine, I finally laid out all the rawness and the hurt in front of Jesus. And without hesitating, He picked it up. Perhaps the answer to following my heart waited with the very One who created my feelings?

Quite by accident, out of desperation, I discovered that Jesus takes all of our deep heart offerings and then speaks love into those holes.

He receives our hearts just as they are—and *then He gives us His.*

What if, instead of choosing to respond or react from our hearts, we *receive* His? What if, instead of following our hearts, we *lead* our hearts to Him?

His holy tending of our deepest places awaits. He will hold our messiness and catch our tears and make us whole again. *(Marnie H. from Ohio)*

Chapter 7

~~THE FUTURE IS FEMALE~~

THE FUTURE IS FOUND TOGETHER

Tears streamed down my cheeks, soaking the front of my cellphone. I could barely believe what I was hearing.

One of my dearest friends, the most selfless, servant-hearted person I knew, told me her husband wanted a divorce. We loved them as a couple. We loved their kids like our own. And now, the thought of them not being together made me terribly sad—more than that, it made me mad.

This woman was a role model to me when it came to being a wife who consistently cared about her husband and put his needs above her own. She always thought about her children and made sure they were taken care of. Yet, because Satan planted clever lies in her husband's mind, which fostered sin, and he didn't do the deep work of healing from past pain, he began to resent my friend, blaming her for everything that wasn't as it should be in his life. I was angry because of how she was being treated, but more so, I was mad at the enemy.

Only a few years earlier, this same friend prayed diligently for me when I thought my marriage was headed toward divorce. She stood in the gap for me when all I could do was weep and cry out to God for rescue. Now, regardless of the outcome in her marriage, I wanted to do what I could for her.

Unfortunately, this is a common storyline in our culture. Marriages around the world are being assaulted relentlessly, regardless of whether the spouses are believers or not. Combine this attack with society's fixation on self and making your heart happy, and it's the perfect storm.

Satan hates connected hearts. He despises unity. He purposefully separates himself from everything loving or selfless because pride and self-centeredness are key components to his plan. He thrives on putting to death life-giving relationships, first with God and then with others. That's why he regularly breaks apart the bond found within the beauty of marriage.

We will talk about the cultural and biblical relationships between men and women within this chapter, but first we need to understand why the enemy struck at the earliest union between man and woman so fiercely.

The answer can be discovered in Eden.

A Match Made in Eden

God created light, land, water, vegetation, and animals all before forming man because humanity was called to reign over what the Creator had made. And yet, God held off on making the woman. He made both males and females for all the animal species. Why did He wait to make Eve?

"Then the LORD God said, 'It is not good for the man to be alone. I will make a helper who is just right for him'" (Gen. 2:18). Immediately we receive a glimpse of God's compassion, as well as His concerns. Loneliness was not part of God's original plan. God Himself was never alone. The three People in the Trinity are continually connected to each other, unified in *glory, purpose,* and *importance.* Human beings, who are made in

God's image, are no different. The man needed someone who was right for him, someone who would understand him, someone who was intentionally designed to be his equal in *glory, purpose,* and *importance.*

After creating all the animals, God brought each one before the man to name. This wasn't done because God was perplexed in trying to find Adam's match. The Lord knew exactly what was going to happen. Instead, it was for Adam's benefit that He demonstrated how nothing else could make the cut. Only the woman would do.

And so, the woman was formed out of Adam's rib. She was taken from his side as a symbol of significance and similarity. She was meant to stand beside him, not above him or below him. Woman came from man but all mankind would come from woman. The man and the woman would depend on each other to cultivate and create life.

When the man saw the woman, his heart recognized the magnitude of the moment. Here she was, the one he was hoping for! Flesh of his flesh, (literal) bone of his bone. She was right for him in every single way. They were two unique creations who were made to be united. And they were both individual reflections of God's image.

The Bible says, "The man and his wife were both naked, but they felt no shame" (Gen. 2:25). This speaks to the full meaning of being seen and accepted. Shame, blame, and fear were nonexistent. Instead, they appreciated each other and saw each other through the eyes of God. They were equally respected. Equally important. Equally loved and cherished by the Father and each other.

From this foundation man and woman were called to multiply, take dominion, and rule as one. They both were given the same mission and command by their Creator.

But there's another dimension to marriage even more destructive to the devil's plan to divide, and it happened *after* the fall in the garden. With the entrance of sin came an opportunity to display the redeeming power of the gospel in all its splendor, particularly within marriage.

Why Marriage to Eve Makes the Enemy Mad

On his own, man is made in the image of God, but his existence alone does not tell the story of redemption. Only after Eve was created can we see the longing in Adam's heart for human connection fulfilled, a longing similar to the one God has for us who are separated from Him because of our sin.

God made Eve as a partner for Adam and gave her a specific name that highlights an important aspect of God's character. Eve is called man's *ezer kenegdo*, his "lifesaver."[1] She literally foreshadows the rescuing heart of our Savior as the hero. In English these words are translated *helper*, but the term has been downgraded from the depth of its true meaning.

Out of the twenty-one times *ezer* is used in the Old Testament, sixteen are used to describe YHWH and the way God rescues His people.[2] "Happy are you, O Israel! Who is like you, a people saved by the LORD, the shield of your *help*, and the sword of your triumph! Your enemies shall come fawning to you, and you shall tread upon their backs" (Deut. 33:29 ESV). As we can see in this Scripture, *ezer* is a military term implying "an active intervention on behalf of someone. It describes someone who is committed to your well-being to the extent that s/he is willing to die or kill for you."[3] To label wives as an assistant or a servant to husbands clearly misses the warrior heart woven into women by God.

With *helper*'s true importance in mind, we can understand why Eve was a threat to the dominion of darkness. The serpent went after the woman in order to take the entire God-ordained operation down. And at first, it probably appeared like he succeeded. The pure relationship between Adam and Eve became tainted instantly, the moment they ate the fruit. Shame and blame came pouring from their lips and suddenly their nakedness wasn't something to be desired but feared. Sin caused a separation between God and humanity and also husband and wife.

To the woman God said, "Your desire will be for your husband, and he shall rule over you" (Gen. 3:16 NASB). After creating both Adam and Eve, "God blessed *them*; and God said to *them*, 'Be fruitful and multiply, and fill the earth, and *subdue it*; and *rule over* the fish of the sea and over the birds of the sky and over every living thing that moves on the earth'" (Gen. 1:28 NASB). God gave this calling to both the man and the woman. Yet, because of the effects of the fall, a battle for control would occur. Instead of fighting against the enemy united, they would fight against each other divided.

It's interesting to note that God pronounced a prophetic consequence over Adam and Eve, but only Satan received a permanent curse. This is because redemption was already at play for God's children.

When sin entered the picture, the Father wasn't surprised. Scripture says that "even before he made the world, God loved us and chose us in Christ to be holy and without fault in his eyes" (Eph. 1:4 NLT). This means before any human stepped foot on our planet, God decided to make us clean in Christ and redeem humanity's choice to sin. Jesus was coming for His bride before she was brought into existence. He sacrificed His life before Adam and Eve took matters into their own hands. The way Jesus loves the church shows His faithfulness to restore.

As believers, if we put Jesus at the center of our marriages, He will work out the most beautiful love story that paints a picture of His passion. I was looking at the word *together* the other day and noticed something quite brilliant. I realized we can dissect *together* into three separate words. TO. GET. HER. The purpose of bringing a man and woman *together* is to highlight the picture of Christ pursuing His bride, the church. God did everything to bring us back to Himself by laying down His life so we could live. Jesus paid the highest price *to get her*—to rescue us, His beloved.

Marriage is a powerful portrayal of the gospel, inviting humanity to experience unconditional and covenantal love between God and His people.

Adam and Eve demonstrate the gospel first to each other and then to the world. This makes the enemy furious.

If Satan went after Adam's bride, we can be certain he will continue to attack Christ's bride too. But there's always good news when we have Jesus. We serve a God who fights for us and wins. "For the Lord your God is the One who is going with you, to fight for you against your enemies, to save you" (Deut. 20:4 NASB).

Jesus protects His church, and just like God weaves warriorhood into men and women, He puts His protective heart into His people, particularly husbands. Men are commanded to guard and care for their wives. We all can feel a holy defensiveness rise when someone messes with those we love. But I've seen an extra share of this protective nature in my boys.

My middle son, Nathan, and I can be immersed in a lightsaber battle and Daddy will slide into the fight too. The moment Madison starts attacking me, Nathan goes into crazy defense mode and starts battling his dad. It's like clockwork. Why? Because I am the most important woman in his life right now, and I believe God has wired this drive to protect me (and one day his wife) for a good and gospel-centered purpose. Christ fought for His beloved at the cross and He continues to do so every day.

Regardless of the enemy's attempt to break apart any unity between men and women, God's children continue to proclaim the death and resurrection of Jesus and they do so in similar yet different ways.

Redefining the Roles

With all the conversation surrounding gender and identity in our culture, it's easy to fall into the mindset that men and women are basically the same. But when we take away our distinctiveness, we also take away God's divine design. We all have the same calling to be disciples in Christ, yet Eve was not modeled as Adam's clone. She is her own being and set apart for things she was made to do. God made men and women to be different, but it's not only in biology.

I grew up with three sisters and one brother. Now I am a boy mama to three wonderful boys. But I can tell you, there's often a stark difference between young boys and girls. While we are equal in value and righteousness in Christ and should be treated with the same dignity and honor in society (not abused or under oppressive leadership as some are), God created us in a manner that offers balance and beauty while presenting His characteristics.

If man is described as the head in marriage, then woman can be seen as the heart. I'm not talking about men being more logical or women being more in touch with their feelings. Both men and women are rational and emotional. But many women have a unique ability to see the needs of those around them and, like the physical heart, a woman nurtures those in her care with vital nutrients including love, compassion, wisdom, and empathy. She circulates them into the system and helps everyone thrive. Physically speaking, without the heart, the entire body couldn't function, including the head.

Although there's much debate on women's roles within the church, it's clear that women play an important part in building the kingdom. They were the first to proclaim the good news after Christ's resurrection. They were (and are) filled with the same Holy Spirit who empowered the original disciples on the day of Pentecost. Paul sent a woman to represent him as his messenger when he wrote to the church in Rome, which is arguably the most important letter he ever wrote.

Women have been judges, prophets, leaders, and evangelists in Scripture, and this is not because God accidentally assigned them. God ordains all of His people to be exactly where they need to be for His glory. He doesn't make mistakes when it comes to the mission field.

The enemy loves to create division regarding women's roles in the church, but true unity is found when we focus on the *kingdom roles* of men and women.

Above all else, women are called to be disciples of Christ. This comes above being a wife, mother, daughter, coworker, or friend. As we will see later in this book, living as a disciple and making disciples needs to be the hallowed rhythm pulsing through our veins.

Now if everyone seriously looked at what is required from godly leaders, both in the home and in the church, they may be a little more hesitant to want the role. Within marriage, a man as the leader is called to love his wife like Christ loves the church, literally to the point of laying down his life for her. This dying involves more than physical death; it encapsulates putting the needs and desires of the wife above his own. He dies to himself daily, choosing service over control.

Like Jesus, the husband washes her feet and also washes her in the truth of who she is in Christ. He blesses her, prays for her, takes care of her, partners with her, supports her, considers her, honors her, protects her, loves her, does everything that is necessary to bring her abundant life and freedom. This is not an easy task because the leader is also held accountable for the well-being of those he is leading.

In the church, being a biblical leader should never be about power and position. Instead, those who participate in leading a congregation are responsible for pouring love and truth into the people God has entrusted to them. If they are not cultivating an atmosphere that makes men *and* women feel safe, seen, and secure, then they are not following the Lord's footsteps. Christ needs to be the central character in His church, not celebrity pastors or preachers.

We can learn a lot from David and Saul, two kings of Israel. David was a tender of sheep. Saul was a seeker of fame. David was a man after God's heart. Saul was a man after his own heart. David influenced others to worship the Lord. Saul influenced others to worship self.

The leaders God ordains should be humble shepherds versus powerful figures. Michelle Lee-Barnewall's book *Neither Complementarian nor Egalitarian* talks about the radical reversal of Christ's kingdom-minded culture within the church. She says,

> Christ demonstrates not only service but also the way in which those with status are especially called upon to renounce their worldly privileges and rights and reverse the expectations of personal gain from their position. The end result of such actions is not the expected disorder and chaos but love and unity as Paul calls all believers, and leaders most of all, to imitate Christ in this way.[4]

In essence, leaders place greater priority on the common good and growth of others than their own, which inspires others to follow in unity. If this was the mindset of those called to lead their flocks and families, following their lead would come much more naturally and leaders would feel the weight more heavily. Adam would be submitted to God's heart, which has always honored and elevated Eve.

Unfortunately, abuses in power do occur within the body of Christ and culture as a whole. As a disclaimer, if you or someone you love is being abused, personal boundaries of safety are essential and should be talked about with trusted friends or professionals. It breaks the heart of God to see His children treated wrongfully, and He is there with you to comfort you. One day you will experience healing in the midst of the pain, and because of this truth we can put the destructiveness of the past or present behind us. It doesn't have to determine our future.

If we have been hurt by harsh and unfair treatment, it doesn't mean we need to retaliate in kind. By saying *the future is female*, we are negating half of humanity, echoing the same mistreatment that has been done to women for centuries. I understand the desire to embolden and inspire through this statement, but biblically, God's children need one another.

Uplifting women should not facilitate the downfall of men. This would only feed the enemy's schemes to divide and conquer when we should be conquering Satan together as one. The devil wants us to believe that in order to empower women we need to separate ourselves from men. But God makes it clear—a united front wins the war.

The Future Is Ours

One of my favorite couples in Scripture is Priscilla and Aquila, a married missionary couple Paul met while in Corinth. The couple's names are always paired together, interestingly often with the wife's name coming first. Some believe this is because she was well-off financially or she was the superior teacher in the relationship, thus Paul gave her preference.[5] A smaller group of scholars argue Priscilla may have been the author of Hebrews.[6] Regardless of the details, the two were the model of a unified partnership for the gospel of Christ. Paul called them "coworkers" because both played central roles in teaching, equipping, and ministering to the churches in Corinth, Ephesus, and Rome.

What I love most about Priscilla and Aquila is their single focus on building the kingdom. Their minds were on the mission and they gained a grand reputation for their work. Paul writes to the church in Rome telling them to greet Priscilla and Aquila, "who risked their necks for my life, to whom not only I give thanks but all the churches of the Gentiles give thanks as well" (Rom. 16:4 ESV).

This is a high compliment for a union used by God. And it gives us hope for restored Eden-like relationships between men and women, despite sin and the serpent's influence. We can be connected in the Creator once more.

Satan is selling lies we don't need to buy. We can pursue unity over division and choose to see our relationships with each other from our Maker's perspective. We can celebrate our gifts, and even our differences as men and women, because diversity helps humanity reflect the whole personhood of God. Every believer has a unique and indispensable role in spreading the good news.

I need to tell you about the awkward time my oldest son became an evangelist. David is autistic, which results in him speaking his mind freely, sometimes to a fault. On Halloween a few years ago, we decided to go to Chick-fil-A after trick-or-treating. David was looking around the restaurant and became fascinated with a man whose face was painted green in order to look like a zombie. We have told our kids we will not be dressing up as scary characters because we want to show people how Jesus is love and life. David remembered this and before we could stop him he approached this complete stranger and started asking questions.

"Why are you wearing green on your face?"

"It's Halloween and I'm supposed to be a zombie."

"Do you know Jesus?"

"Yes! Jesus is one of my favorite people."

"Then why are you dressed like someone who is bad?"

The man was speechless and so were we! It was an awkward and awestruck moment. I didn't apologize for my son's questions. They were honest and curious, but the words of children can be incredibly convicting.

"Well, buddy, you're right. I don't know why I'm dressed like this."

Five minutes later we saw him come out of the bathroom with his face wiped clean. Our families exchanged numbers and within one week this complete stranger was baptized into a new life with Christ! All because God chose to use our "different" son to reach someone searching for Him.

I say this because diversity among God's people should be viewed positively, and this includes how God has fashioned men and women. I'm able to see the beauty in how my son is made and I know God is using him. In the same way, we can acknowledge differences in how men and women are made and still know God will use both for His kingdom.

The Spirit indwells and fills God's people equally, not giving preference to anyone based on gender. We all have access to the same degree of help and empowerment from God. He is the One who decides how He wants to reveal Himself to others through us, according to His wisdom and will.

When we choose to partner with others—whether we are married, engaged, or single—we agree to support the gifts the Holy Spirit has imparted to each disciple of Christ, trying our best not to limit them out of fear or man-made conditions. We need to be careful to read God's Word in context and seek to understand the author's true meaning in any passage in Scripture. We may not agree on every issue, but we can decide to fix our eyes on Jesus because true unity is grounded in Him.

The future isn't female or male, Greek or Jew, slave or free, or any other distinction that can be used to divide. Instead, heaven will consist of every tribe and tongue praising Christ in harmony under His lordship.

Jesus is coming for His bride. Together we wait expectantly for our future and look forward to the promise of relationships made right. The gospel story is still being told. And we have the privilege of showing God's goodness as we lead one another toward Love.

Stories from Sisters Who Believed HE Could

CASEY'S STORY:

I married my opposite. The artist and the engineer. He's a numbers and spreadsheets kind of guy and I'm a paint-flowers-on-the-wall-because-it's-a-Tuesday kind of girl.

God created us to be uniquely two—raised by different parents, with different strengths and weaknesses, different life experiences and backgrounds, different interests and hobbies, and different goals. But then we fell in love. Through our vows before God, we're united as one.

What happens when two very different individuals get married and have to adult together? Raise kids? Make budgets? Maintain a home together? Make big life decisions? Serve together?

Early in our marriage we went canoeing. It was his first time, but I grew up paddling in the bayou. Typically, the more experienced canoer sits in the back to steer unless the other paddler is bigger and stronger. I took the seat in front. It was my job to warn of any obstacles in the way. It didn't take long before I, sweating and frustrated, began to steer. With the two of us steering, we got caught up in the brush of the bank, ran into fallen trees and sandbars, and found ourselves facing upstream when we were supposed to go down.

So, I did what any other free spirit would do: I jumped out of the canoe. He didn't have time to calculate his counterbalance. The canoe flipped and landed bottom side up. Frustration switched to laughter as we pulled the canoe to the bank to climb aboard and start again. This time we worked together. We kept pace with each other. I navigated, he steered, and together we synced our strokes.

Our canoe trip taught us that we're only opposites when we fight against the current. By God's design, it takes the strength of two to make it down the bayou. (*Casey H. from Louisiana*)

Part 2

. . . So She Did

Living Out the Truths of the Gospel in Christ

Chapter 8

YOU CAN SLAY ALL DAY

When I was single I felt the Lord calling me to do missions work overseas. I have to laugh when I think about this because ten years earlier I begged God to *never* make me a missionary. The thought of leaving my friends and family made my heart ache.

You can imagine my hesitation when I felt the tug to tell university students about Jesus on the other side of the world in Australia. It was literally the farthest I could be from home. When I told my dad, he was sad because he's a loving man who values the closeness of family. But as I studied Scripture, I saw how God continually called His children to unknown lands or sent them far away as messengers of the good news. Now Jesus was asking me.

After wrestling with the Lord over my call, I traveled to Colorado for a conference to meet the wonderful ministry team I would be living with for a year or more. It was surreal envisioning my life on the other side of the planet, away from everything I had known and loved, except Jesus. In the midst of God's glorious mountains, I decided to walk down by a small river running between the towering trees near our hotel. As I sat on the rocks and watched the water rush past my feet, I reached down to touch the cool, refreshing stream.

I asked God for the strength to be able to leave everyone behind for the sake of the gospel. I asked Him to help me do the one thing I begged Him not to make me do. In those hushed moments I felt the presence of God surround me in the wonder of His creation. It seemed as though He was reaching down, enveloping me in His nature as a reminder that I would never be alone. No matter where I would travel, no matter what He would ask me to do, the Spirit of the living God would always be near. His presence wasn't just around me, He was in me, empowering me to do the hard and hallowed things on my consecrated path.

Water is often used in association with God throughout the Bible and it's no real surprise. All living things need water to survive. And where water is present, life exists also.[1]

The apostle John recited the words of Jesus when He said, "Anyone who is thirsty may come to me! Anyone who believes in me may come and drink! For the Scriptures declare, 'Rivers of living water will flow from his heart'" (John 7:37–38). This is the eternal water that sustains, and it is called *living*. When Jesus says *living*, He implies more than a trickle. It's an ever-flowing river whose powerful current surges from our almighty God. His living water pours out from heaven into the depths of our hearts, and then overflows into those we encounter in life. And the real kicker? This water is given in *equal* amounts to all who believe.

Centuries earlier, another woman walked by a river in Philippi. She was a wealthy woman who sold luxurious purple cloth, which by their culture's standards meant she was successful at *slaying all day*. Although Lydia was a God-worshiper, she hadn't been transformed yet by the power of the gospel. Her soul thirsted for the truth as she watched the river run by.

One day Paul and Silas began to talk with the women at the water and Lydia took notice. Scripture says, "The Lord opened her heart to pay attention" (Acts 16:14 ESV), and in the next few moments she went from hearing to believing to being filled with the living water her spirit craved. Soon her whole household became believers in Jesus and were baptized into their new faith.

This strong and established woman became a prominent part of the church in Philippi, hosting disciples like Paul and Silas in her home (Acts 16:40 NASB). She was called to minister where the Lord had placed her, even if it meant risking her business, reputation, or life. Lydia was a friend to missionaries like me.

I think about my time in Colorado often, sitting on the banks of God's river like my friend Lydia. Little did I know my team going to Australia would fall apart while we were raising support. Instead of my heading to Australia for a couple years, the Lord sent me back to my alma mater, the University of Iowa. I didn't understand why Jesus would call me toward one thing, only to switch things up a few months later.

Following Christ can feel a lot like a river with its turns and sudden dips. The ebb and flow can change directions, but God continues to ask us to trust His process as He cultivates an open posture of "here I am, send me."

Whether we are sent to our neighborhoods, workplaces, homes, or distant lands, Jesus doesn't ask us to go without giving us the greatest form of empowerment we will ever need—the Holy Spirit of God.

The Spirit is the number one way we encounter Christ's enablement, so much so that Jesus told His disciples it would be better for them if He was no longer present because someone else would take His place. I'm sure the disciples thought no one was better than Jesus. But apparently, it wasn't the case. This coming One would never depart from them. He would be joined to the everlasting part of who they are.

"Nevertheless, I tell you the truth: it is to your advantage that I go away, for if I do not go away, the Helper will not come to you. But if I go, I will send him to you" (John 16:7 ESV). This verse is powerful because it shows us how the Holy Spirit has a calling too, and Jesus is the One sending Him.

The Spirit's assignment is the sanctification and strengthening of the saints. He is our assured Helper, giving us the capacity to walk through life while following in the footsteps of Christ. *The Spirit's calling is to help us carry out our calling,* and He promises to do so until the very end.

From Shaking to Unshaken

Jesus' last words included the Great Commission, which was a big task. "Therefore, go and make disciples of all the nations, baptizing them in the name of the Father and the Son and the Holy Spirit. Teach these new disciples to obey all the commands I have given you. And be sure of this: I am with you always, even to the end of the age" (Matt. 28:19–20). And then Jesus leaves. Oh, the irony . . .

I can only imagine what the disciples were feeling. They had just witnessed the death and resurrection of their trusted Rabbi and now He disappears again. He's with them, then not, with them, then not. By the time Jesus ascended into heaven, they were probably confused and frightened. They knew what happened when you went against the religious system. They saw how Rome handled troublemakers. And now Jesus was asking them to do the very thing that got Him killed.

From here, the disciples returned to the upper room of the house where they were staying and prayed. Jesus also said before He left, "*You will receive power when the Holy Spirit comes upon you.* And you will be my witnesses, telling people about me everywhere—in Jerusalem, throughout Judea, in Samaria, and to the ends of the earth" (Acts 1:8). Jesus told them to stay in Jerusalem until the Father sent the gift He promised (vv. 4–5). And so we have more than 120 followers of Christ, including the disciples and women who followed Jesus' ministry, gathered in one place. Together they were hiding and hoping for this Helper.

I wish I was present for what happened next. The sound of

a powerful windstorm filled the room and could be heard in the surrounding area. Devout Jews from different nations came running to see what was happening. Figures resembling flames descended on all who were present, men and women alike, as they were permanently filled with the Holy Spirit. Then they began speaking in other languages, tongues these devout Jews could understand because each one heard their native language. Can you picture the sight?

Divine enabling for the children of God had arrived and on this day the fellowship of 120 grew by three thousand! These uncertain followers were no longer shaking but *unshaken*. They were emboldened to do what Jesus commissioned them to do—to be witnesses telling people about Christ to the ends of the earth.

You have this fire of God inside of you too.

The same Spirit who empowered trembling believers resides in your heart, ready to move and work if you are willing. God's power was not reserved for the early church. It's alive and active in those who believe and are surrendered to His plan. God is the same today, tomorrow, and yesterday, which means the Holy Spirit and His ability has not changed either.

This fire is a form of power only sourced in the Spirit, not through any human skill. God's power has been referenced in the Bible as *dunamis*, a Greek word meaning "power, force, or ability."[2] It's also the root for the word *dynamite* and was used more than one hundred times in the New Testament.[3] Although the *dunamis* power of God often pertains to Jesus and His miraculous works, the term is also used to highlight the power behind the miracles and movement of Christ's followers. Jesus promised the Spirit's *dunamis* would hold unstoppable authority and would never be taken away.

And yet, many people diminish the work of the Holy Spirt, either because they are not familiar with the third person of the Trinity or they have concerns regarding His capability. My relationship with God reflected this mindset for more than half of my Christian walk.

After I chose to follow Jesus, I tried putting limits on what the Spirit could do, even though it didn't change who He was or what He could accomplish. When I witnessed something outside the realm of my comfort, I brushed it off as something never applicable to me or my ordinary life.

But God loves using our "ordinary" in extraordinary ways. His power shines through the fissures and faults we think exclude us from being used for His glory. I realized defining the Spirit's ability based on *my* perception of what was acceptable actually hindered the ways God wanted to use and transform me.

I had to ask myself what I was afraid of. The fact that these miracles I was seeing were happening, or that I didn't think any miracle could happen for me? God gently showed me it was the latter.

The Spirit is not fractioned off among believers, where some get more of Him while others receive less. We all receive the same Helper. The same authority and aid exists for each person in God's family, but the Spirit decides which spiritual gifts we receive.

In 1 Corinthians, Paul devotes three chapters to addressing the different gifts of the Spirit, which are meant to glorify God, spread the good news, and build up God's growing church. Each gift is equal in importance, with every member as significant as the next. Sometimes we can look at other people's gifts and devalue our own contribution to the kingdom.

Gifts like evangelism, teaching, prophecy, and leadership are highlighted on the center stage, while other gifts like serving, giving, exhortation, and administration happen behind the curtain. In the eyes of the Lord, however, all are needed in order to keep the body of Christ flourishing and functioning.

Our knowledge of God will continue to grow as long as we press in and let the Spirit speak and teach, even if we're confused or cautious.

Otherwise, our doubts may downplay demonstrations of God's power when the range of His works should result in praise.

As the psalmist writes, "The LORD has done great things for us; we are glad" (Ps. 126:3 ESV). Let's be grateful for God's incomparable *dunamis* within.

How to Slay on the Hard Days

It's one thing to know we have the Spirit inside of us, but how do we as disciples live empowered by Him and experience this "dynamite" daily, especially when it gets hard?

First, it's important to understand that free will doesn't apply solely to sinning and salvation. It also applies to our sanctification and submission to the Spirit.

We can live empowered by our self or the Spirit, but we can't do both. The decision lies with us. We choose whether we will allow God access to every part of our being, even the areas we try to hide out of shame, pride, or sin. Jesus wants all of us. Our desire to hold back creates a tension every person will encounter when trying to walk in step with the Spirit. Human nature veers toward pioneering our own path versus allowing the Lord to determine our course.

But when we finally choose to open our hands, we'll find that yielding to the Father's sufficiency and strength actually brings immense relief. Pushing and pulling our way into our plans creates self-induced pressure, *but a surrendered heart allows God to clear the path.* He is the One whose strength is greater and whose knowledge is always wiser.

Another key aspect to living empowered by the Spirit is to place our desired outcomes at the foot of the cross, particularly if the circumstances don't meet our (or others') expectations. God is really good at being our Redeemer, especially when we don't receive the answer we're looking for. But having our prayers answered the way *we* think is best isn't the goal of our relationship with God. Abiding with Him in the midst of our pain and prayers is.

The act of abiding is equivalent to cultivating our union with the Creator, and it's the most personal aspect of the Holy Spirit's work.

In John 15, the apostle uses one word repeatedly, which is translated in two different ways, depending on the translation you're reading. What I love about these two words is how they both portray the full meaning behind what Jesus was saying to His disciples regarding godly connection: "Remain/Abide in Me, and I in you. Just as the branch cannot bear fruit of itself but must remain/abide in the vine, so neither can you unless you remain/abide in Me" (John 15:4 NASB/ESV)

When we talk about *remaining,* it's about proximity. Like Mary at the feet of Jesus, we forget about everything else, and stay near Him. We allow Christ to carry us close to His heart. We rest by His side, listen to His words, and choose to settle our souls permanently in Him.

When we talk about *abiding,* it's about unity. We have a meaningful relationship with Jesus that can't be severed. We are in Christ and He is in us. His thoughts become our own and His Word becomes our bread. Every spiritual blessing we have results from our union with the Son.

Both words imply connection and communion, but together they cover what it truly means to be a humble branch attached to the Vine. As the branch is nourished by the Vine, it develops and produces fruit from the Spirit like love, joy, peace, patience, kindness, goodness, faithfulness, gentleness, and self-control—all of which can be demonstrated in various ways throughout our lives (Gal. 5:22–23).

Abiding in Christ is a requirement for real growth, and it's the only way we can face the hard days with confidence in God. Christ's personal nurturing makes it possible to press forward.

If we want to *slay all day,* we need to make sure we *stay* connected to Christ. Whether it's through prayer, worship, community, Bible reading, or spending time in His presence, our souls need more of Him in order to get through the long weeks. The Spirit is our lifeline to God.

Spending consistent time with God cannot leave a person untouched. As a busy mom, I know how unfeasible it is to have extended periods of time to yourself, which makes being alone with Jesus basically nonexistent. Most of the time I feel as though if I'm not taking care of the little humans, I'd be staring at a wall out of pure exhaustion.

But the Spirit doesn't need solo time or substantial amounts of time to refresh our souls. All He desires is an invitation to minister to us in the myriad of our daily moments, in small but significant ways. He wants us to be open to receive and hear from Him.

The Spirit can speak to us through different means, but all are meant to renew our minds with His truth, which results in freedom from hurt, lies, and sin. When we're willing to let the Spirit convict, challenge, encourage, and edify us in Christ, our lives will not look the same as the day we decided to follow Jesus. We will walk confidently as new creations toward the throne of God where "we will receive his mercy, and we will find grace to help us when we need it most" (Heb. 4:16).

Slaying with the God of the Impossible

When I was a new mom I decided to try to motivate myself to exercise by signing up for a half marathon in Disney World. It sounded like a good plan at the time, but there was no way I was going to run thirteen miles by myself. So I did what any oldest sister would do—I convinced my three sisters to run it with me.

Training was going okay up until the week before we were scheduled to leave for the race. I woke up in the middle of the night in debilitating pain that made it difficult to limp, let alone run. We immediately went to the ER.

After some tests, they discovered I'd burst an ovarian cyst. When I told the doctor I was going to be running a half marathon in four days, he said, "No, you're not." I was in tears, but it wasn't because of the pain. My entire family, including my parents and my siblings' significant others, was flying down to watch us run, and one of the boyfriends was going to propose at the finish line. It was a moment I couldn't miss. I started this whole thing and now I had to finish it.

The doctor gave me permission to *attempt* to run the race, and that was all I needed—a chance. I asked God to empower me to make it to the end so I could see my sister say yes. We ran for two minutes and walked for two minutes almost the entire run. My sisters easily could have darted ahead of me, but they stayed by my side to support me and spur me onward. I prayed with each step and fixed my mind on the proposal. Although I was tired and the ache lingered throughout the race, by God's grace I crossed the finish line with my sisters and witnessed a real-life fairy-tale ending.

Only God, my friend. And the persevering power of the Holy Spirit.

When we allow the Spirit to work in us, there is nothing too big He can't do. God honors the efforts we put into the process, but He is the power behind the results. Clearly, in my case, I couldn't do it on my own. My scenario was the opposite of culture's "I've got this" mentality. The doctor told me I couldn't and shouldn't. I had my determination but depending on God is what helped me reach the race's end.

The Holy Spirit has the ability to change what we never thought was possible, both in ourselves and our circumstances. He is the One who helps transform us into the image of God's Son, not the image of society. The Spirit reminds us to obey God's commands regarding our character and choices. He is the Comforter who carries our burdens when our souls are swallowed in grief. He reveals what God wants us to see in Scripture and speaks to others through us on God's behalf. He is always at work, always ready to fill, always ready to bring about God's promises.

Honestly, the benefits we have as believers because of the Holy

Spirit could fill this entire book. It's safe to say Jesus was right. It *was* better for Him to return to heaven because the Spirit saves us from having to handle life's adversities alone.

The Power of Walking Secure and Sealed

When I think of seals, I immediately think of the red wax stamp Mr. Darcy put on his letter as he defended his honor to Elizabeth Bennet. The drama of eighteenth-century love stories is hard to miss. Seals are still used today on envelopes, contracts, or other important documents in order to prove ownership. The seal guaranteed the contents of the document were from the person whose seal was presented.[4] Paul is familiar with the significance of seals too. He tells believers in Ephesus, "In him you also, when you heard the word of truth, the gospel of your salvation, and believed in him, *were sealed with the promised Holy Spirit*" (Eph. 1:13 ESV). But he doesn't stop there.

In another letter Paul writes to the church at Corinth, saying, "It is God who enables us, along with you, to stand firm for Christ. He has commissioned us, and he has identified us as his own by placing the Holy Spirit in our hearts as the first installment that guarantees everything he has promised us" (2 Cor. 1:21–22). Our seal may not be as glamorous as Mr. Darcy's because it is unseen, but it is the most important seal anyone will ever receive. The seal of the Holy Spirit proves we belong to the Lord and it serves as a guarantee of what's to come. Even if the waters start to get wild, being sealed in Christ secures our steps.

A lot of people love the scene in the Bible where Peter walks on water to Jesus. It's pretty impressive, but there's another scene involving Peter, Jesus, and water that's even more moving and it happens after Christ's resurrection.

The night of Christ's betrayal, Peter promised he would never abandon Jesus, but just as the Lord predicted, Peter ended up denying Jesus not once, but three times. He did the thing he never thought he would do.

This is typically where Satan jumps in and reminds us of our shortcomings and how the Son of God will surely reject us for committing never-will-I-ever sins. It's a common tape he plays on repeat for all the saints. But Jesus rectified man's slavery to sin through His sacrifice and He comes to find us, especially when we feel like our seal's been broken.

After rising from the dead, Jesus pursued Peter again.

At this point Peter went back to his old life as a fisher by the sea because he didn't feel worthy to fish for men. But Christ didn't want to reject Peter; He wanted to restore him. The Savior found Peter and a handful of disciples struggling to catch a single fish after fishing for the entire night. Reentry was not going as planned.

Jesus called out to His disciples from the shoreline, saying, "Children, you do not have any fish to eat, do you?" (John 21:5 NASB), to which they replied no. In a beautifully poetic way, Jesus then restored Peter by righting instances that had previously gone wrong.

Jesus told them to cast their net to the side of the boat and He miraculously filled their net with an abundance of fish, echoing the first encounter where Peter was called to follow Christ. Once Peter realized it was Jesus on the shore, he jumped out of the boat, similar to the time he saw Jesus walking on water. Except this time Peter's eyes were fixed on his Savior, not the surrounding waves. After he had hurriedly swum to shore, the two of them had one of the most significant conversations they would ever have. Jesus asked Peter three times, the same number of times he denied knowing Christ, if he loved Him. After each question, Jesus didn't judge His disciple, He justified him. God personally revealed how this new gospel was one of grace, and the security of Christ's love put the final nail in condemnation's coffin.

If you've ever wondered whether God has removed His seal of belonging from your heart, I encourage you to remember this disciple (whom Jesus renamed the "rock") and how he messed up multiple times. But Peter's feet were secure as He stood on the true Rock of his salvation. When Jesus left for heaven soon thereafter, the sealing of the Holy Spirit made this security all the more sure.

Dear reader, Jesus will not let us be overcome by shame, overwhelm, sin, or fear when the Spirit does His holy work. He is the Sealer of God's sons and daughters. It doesn't matter what others say. It doesn't even matter if we think we're disqualified or unfit. The Lord Himself endorses us and has commissioned us as His disciples. He puts His seal of legitimacy behind who we are and what God's called us to do.

Maybe He'll ask you to jump out of the boat and into the waves. Or maybe He'll help you walk on water. Regardless, the Spirit of the living God will empower you with strength as you step out in faith and *slay*.

Stories from Sisters Who Believed HE Could

HEATHER'S STORY:

Divorce was something foreign, never an option. How had it become my reality? The glass ball I knew as my life had just been tossed from an overpass onto the busy highway below, and I was scrambling to pick up the shattered pieces as each oncoming vehicle smashed them even more. This could not be *my* life.

God had always been my protector, guiding me away from disaster. How could He let this happen? I cried out in desperation but only heard silence.

God was with me throughout my life, but was I with Him? I had drifted toward my own ways. As the reality of my circumstances set in, I knew I couldn't survive this on my own. I couldn't see clearly or take even one thought captive. I was spiraling out of control and needed God more than ever as I cried out from my pit of despair.

I had few words to offer, uttering only the name of Jesus. Romans 8:26 assures us the Holy Spirit helps in our weakness and the Spirit Himself intercedes with groanings too deep for words when we don't know what to pray.

After wrestling with darkness for seven days and a cry of full surrender, I felt the Spirit's intercession lift and steady me, putting Psalm 40:2 into action. "He lifted me out of the pit of despair, out of the mud and the mire. He set my feet on solid ground and steadied me as I walked along."

God's Word became my every defense as the Holy Spirit revealed truth to my heart and comforted my soul. We slayed the darkness hand in hand as the Spirit empowered me to move from barely surviving to thriving.

Every step was strengthened as I learned life in His presence was far better than anything I could imagine on my own. Through the guidance of the Holy Spirit, I was able to stand up, straighten my crown, and walk forward again grounded in truth. (*Heather J. from Maryland*)

Chapter 9

WE ARE WOMEN OF THE WAY: SPREADING THE GOSPEL LIKE JESUS

Can I tell you about one of the most obvious divine appointments I've experienced? It all started with me saying no to God.

I was flying home from Savannah, Georgia, after spending five marvelous days with fellow Christian writers. My hour layover was in DC but everything was running on time. No worries there.

I walked to the bagel shop and was about to buy my bagel when I felt God prompt me to buy food for the next person in line too. For some reason, fear took over. I began to worry what she would think if I offered to pay for her. This wasn't Starbucks where I could anonymously pay for the car behind me. She would see me face-to-face, and what would she do? Too concerned with the possible awkwardness, I decided to pass on God's ask. I said no to the Spirit's nudge, purchased my food, and left.

Meanwhile, back at the gate, the pilot and crew were missing. A few minutes of delay turned into an hour, which meant I would have to sprint to my gate in DC if I was going to make my connecting flight. During the plane ride there, I felt a strong conviction for my refusal to bless a woman who probably needed encouragement that day. *God never prompts us to do something unless purpose is involved.* I repented and asked the Lord to redeem my no by blessing her through someone else, to which I sensed the Spirit say there would be a next time and that I'd be bold and listen.

Little did I know how soon the "next time" would be.

The plane landed and I rushed down the aisle out of the Jetway. With my laptop, purse, and way too many souvenirs in tow, I dashed my way toward my destination. Why some cruel person built the DC terminals uphill, I don't know, but by the time I arrived at my gate, sweat was pouring out of me like a faucet. In God's good grace (and probably a dash of His humor), my plane was delayed by twenty minutes, which gave me a minute to catch my breath and readjust my flung-about self.

Standing next to me was a young woman whose husband worked for United. We began to chat and she told me she was flying to Chicago urgently because he had just been in an accident. She was nervous about flying into the city at midnight and finding a rental car or an Uber.

And I knew. This was my "next time."

"Listen, I know you just met me, but my husband is coming to pick me up and we are driving right past where you need to go. We would love to give you a ride."

The rest of our time together consisted of me trying to convince her I wasn't a creep, that I loved Jesus and would be honored to serve her if I could. She was a believer, as well as her mother who had been praying God would protect her. She talked with her husband and mom, who both wanted to do a thorough background check on me via socials and my author website, which I completely understood. In the end, God entrusted me to take care of this young woman and keep her safe. We drove her to her husband and prayed for his healing before we left.

It was a much bigger ask than a bagel, and a far greater blessing to be used by God.

Accidental delays didn't exist in this scenario. Everything was perfectly orchestrated by the Master Composer. Multiple prayers converged as the Father heard each cry and answered them in unison through my yes.

How kind is it of Jesus that in the middle of our mess ups He chooses to use those who are willing to be representatives of the gospel—even if He has to repeat His ask a few times?

I want to pose an important question: What do you think is the most loving thing a person can do for another?

We should take care of people's physical needs. We should make sure they are secure, seen, and safe. But if we never tell them about the beauty of the cross, if we never let them know verbally what God has done to bring abundant life and freedom, what good are all the nice works we do? If we never share the gospel, how will they know the Supplier of love and provision?

The most loving thing we can do for another human being is bring them into a relationship with God.

This job isn't reserved for pastors or priests. In fact, Christ specifically chose the original twelve because they were not the religious elite. Yet He deemed them a royal priesthood. These men were everyday people struggling to endure. Christ's disciples were people like you and me. Jesus entrusted His mission to these flawed but faithful followers. And He continues to spread the good news through us today.

Why We Need to Be Women of the Way, Not the World

There was a time I thought saying you were a Christian just meant you had a relationship with Jesus. But the more I've walked through life, the more I've accepted an unfortunate reality.

It's important for us to remember we are not God. We do not

determine whether someone has a relationship with Him or not. We can't look inside a person and see if the Spirit of the living God resides within. But the Bible does leave us with a basic blueprint that highlights the traits of authentic believers.

A difference exists between knowing *about* Jesus and truly *knowing* Jesus. Not all people who say they know Christ are actually Christians. And not all Christians who say they follow Jesus are living as His disciples.

For a long time, I thought believing in what Jesus did on the cross was the extent of living the Christian life. I was a "good kid," but line me up next to my peers in high school and college and you wouldn't have seen a difference between us. I didn't talk about my faith. I didn't stand out from the crowd. I didn't do anything that would make others think I had a relationship with Jesus. And I wanted it that way.

The last thing I wanted was for people to alienate me because I was different from them. I partied and smoked. I dressed in ways that didn't respect my body. I changed the way I talked to match others and went out with guys who were bad for me, some even toxic. I wanted to fit in because standing out was too risky for a girl addicted to approval.

It wasn't until God grabbed hold of my heart in college that I understood what it meant to truly believe in Jesus and live my days as His disciple—to imitate Christ, not the crowd. I began to see the world through God's eyes and realized society's definition of salvation is not the same as Scripture's.

According to a Pew Research Center survey done in 2021, 63 percent of Americans identify as Christians today, a sharp drop from 78 percent in 2007.[1] However, within the number of people who proclaim to be Christian, not everyone lives in a way that aligns with Scripture or the truths Jesus taught. In 2021, George Barna's data discovered that while 51 percent of American adults say they have a "biblical worldview," only 6 percent of American adults actually hold to beliefs historically consistent with a biblical worldview.[2] This means only a sliver of believers stand out the way the disciples stood out for Christ.

Sadly, the research only gets more alarming.

The decline of those who hold a biblical worldview isn't limited to people searching for God. The more dangerous decline is found among those who are shepherding and leading our congregations every week, especially our youth.

As part of the American Worldview Inventory 2022, researchers found that slightly more than a third of pastors in our churches (37 percent) possess a biblical worldview, with the vast majority (62 percent) holding a sort of hybrid view called syncretism.[3] Syncretism blends holistic views, cultural influence, and whatever stance seems most convenient or right to the individual person.[4] According to Barna,

> It's a cut-and-paste approach to making sense of, and responding to life. Rather than developing an internally consistent and philosophically coherent perspective on life, Americans embrace points of view or actions that feel comfortable or seem most convenient. Those beliefs and behaviors are often inconsistent, or even contradictory, but few Americans seemed troubled by those failings.[5]

Christians and church leaders are choosing to believe truths that not only don't make sense, they are unbiblical.

For unbelievers navigating our confusing culture, I can understand why possessing a biblical worldview is irrelevant. Culture worships self, not the Savior. The Bible is not the foundation their lives are built upon. But the pushback from believers when it comes to living according to the entirety of God's Word and way is startling. According to Barna's research, our culture is infiltrating the church more than the church is infiltrating our culture.

Augustine of Hippo once said, "If you believe what you like in the gospels, and reject what you don't like, it is not the gospel you believe, but yourself."[6] When we prioritize and parse out what we feel is relevant in Christianity, we have fashioned the gospel according to man, not God.

My goal in writing this book is to help women avoid the pick-and-choose gospel. If we live as women following the Way of Christ, our personal preferences shouldn't determine what we keep and what we reject. The Bible is not a cafeteria line. It's the inspired Word of God.

Is it healthy to study Scripture and see if certain passages have been misinterpreted? Of course! But deciding to apply parts of Scripture to our lives only if they fit our lifestyle or convenience is not the way Christ tells us to live. Following Jesus means we believe what we read in Scripture because Christ is the Word incarnate. In 2 Timothy we read, "All Scripture is breathed out by God and profitable for teaching, for reproof, for correction, and for training in righteousness" (2 Tim. 3:16 ESV). Scripture is not meant to support our thoughts. It's written to point us toward the mind and heart of God.

We were made to be God's children, part of a family unlike the surrounding landscape. In fact, being different from culture is an appeal to those hurting and wanting help when self-improvement strategies fail. Christians are called to stand strong *and* stand out. Instead, the vast majority have blended in with the philosophies of the world, preaching a gospel Christ Himself did not teach.

Having a biblical worldview means we let God's Word do its full work. We realize it does more than encourage or inspire. It convicts and corrects our wrong doing and thinking. It produces lasting change that emulates the beauty of Christ and makes us look different for Jesus.

As we will see in the next chapter, we have an enemy who wants to prevent people from coming into a saving relationship with Christ and walking in a manner worthy of the gospel, empowered by Him. Many people believe they have a relationship with God. They believe they are good people who are "better off" than those around them. They think they know what God approves of and what He doesn't, views based mainly on the opinions of society, celebrities, or Christian influencers they admire.

But the unfortunate reality is, most people who claim to be Christians do not know the real Jesus because they don't have a relationship with Him, they don't study what's said in Scripture, and they don't want to obey what the Word says. They want the Savior but not the Lord.

We need a spiritual resurrection in our country and world. Barna said it perfectly: "It certainly seems that if America is going to experience a spiritual revival, that awakening is needed just as desperately in our pulpits as in the pews."[7]

And how do we revive the spiritual fervor of believers? Simply making converts won't do. We need to carry out Jesus' final commission before returning to heaven.

We need to go and build a kingdom of Christ-centered disciples.

The Lost Art of Discipleship

Did you know the term *Christian* is used only three times in the Bible? At first, it wasn't used as an identifier among believers, but as a description for unbelievers to classify this new group of people who were breaking through the societal standards.[8] They were called Christians, or "little Christs," in an attempt to define their behaviors and beliefs. They acted like Jesus and did what He did. They were not like the other sects or religions out there. They were clearly set apart.

In Acts 11:26, we see the first mention of the name *Christian* in the town of Antioch, a city set up with intentional walls separating different people groups from one another.[9] And yet, this new group of people defied division and actually unified under the name and leadership of Christ. Following Jesus brought believers together in identity and purpose, something the watching world noticed.

While the term *Christian* wasn't used initially, early believers did use expressions like "followers of the Way" (Acts 9:2; 22:4), disciples, brothers and sisters, children, and saints—words underscoring the importance of connection to Christ and one another. We have been and always will be members of the same chosen family, a community bound together by love.

But today, as we look at ourselves and others who identity as Christians, would we see consistency between how we live our lives and how Jesus lived His? Would we call ourselves "little Christs" or, more importantly, would the unbelieving world see us as such? Do our actions and beliefs really imitate our Lord's, even to the point of suffering and sacrifice?

The first disciples understood the cost. They were hated and disliked by people in charge. They went against the religious systems and, therefore, were judged dangerous. They wouldn't worship government leaders and were persecuted and attacked by Rome. People lost their lives and livelihoods because they believed in Jesus—men, women, and children. And yet, these disciples chose to follow the leading and teachings of Christ, regardless of the religious or societal backdrop.

Being a disciple declares how *Jesus is worth it to us.*

Jesus' death on a cross declares how *we were worth it to Him.*

Once we understand how deeply we are loved . . . how much has been done on our behalf . . . how freely God's grace flows to those who believe . . . we can't help but surrender our lives to the transforming work of His hands.

When I was on staff with Cru (Campus Crusade for Christ), we talked to hundreds of college students about having a relationship with Jesus. Many people said they wanted to know God, but when it came time to let Him change things up, they would back away or return to familiar patterns of living. They were okay with the decision to accept Jesus' gift of salvation, but not okay with becoming a disciple.

But what makes someone a true disciple?

As Jesus sought out the original twelve, He wasn't looking for credentials or charisma. He wanted willing commitment. Jesus needed people who were willing to be *faithful, available,* and *teachable.* These were the characteristics my staff team used while working with college students too. Were they faithful to follow Jesus and show up? Did they make themselves available for time with God and others, as well as His transformation in their hearts? Were they humble enough to allow His teaching to affect all areas of their lives? If the answer to these questions was yes, then we would go all in on discipling.

These questions are not asked with a judgmental attitude. Instead, they're important markers for deciphering whether someone's walk matches that person's talk. Jesus didn't disciple the masses. He deliberately picked and poured into the few. He invested in the faithful ones who followed Him, knowing even then how they would abandon Him in His most desperate hour. He still trusted His disciples to be messengers of the good news.

Although Jesus didn't expect perfection, He did choose men and women willing to let their lives be pruned and purified for the sake of the gospel. We need to copy the Savior's strategy and place discipleship at the center of building God's kingdom. Our churches are suffering and stagnant because of its absence.

The Fruit That Really Counts

Jesus didn't come to make mere converts, He came to make disciples. And He did so in hopes of producing fruit.

Right before Jesus was betrayed by Judas, the Savior spent an extensive amount of time talking to the disciples about staying connected to Him and what it means to be a real disciple. Jesus said, "When you produce much fruit, you are my true disciples. This brings great glory to my Father" (John 15:8). This verse can be misinterpreted to mean we have to do countless good deeds for God in order to be called faithful disciples. But our definition of fruit may be different from our Father's.

The fact that this verse is delivered in the middle of Jesus' teaching regarding staying connected to Him, remaining in His love, and obeying His commands does not point toward the importance of our accomplishments, but rather, the heart behind them.

The fruit that matters the most to God is the cultivation of our character.

Staying connected to Jesus and remaining in His love produces the Christlike fruit that changes how we act. Judas didn't remain in God's truth or love. He walked with the Messiah, witnessed miracles, even performed them himself, and yet he chose greed over the goodness of God.

Character and commitment are the qualities that count and change the world. When we combine character, commitment, and Christ-centered empowerment, a multiplying effect will transpire and the gates of hell will not prevail.

A few years ago, we homeschooled our kids and I attempted to teach my kids math. My second son, Nathan, was a natural, jumping quickly from addition to multiplication. At first, it was difficult for him to see how the multiplication sign was different from addition. Two plus ten was not the same as two times ten. The initial numbers were identical but the principles were different. *Multiplication meant more.* Jesus was natural with math as well. He understood how different principles behind discipleship could produce more power and fruit.

Addition is linear.

But multiplication can be exponential.

Let's do the spiritual math. Jesus poured into the twelve and on just the day of Pentecost three thousand came to faith in Christ. The momentum continued as believers discipled other believers and they preached the good news to the lost. Spiritual multiplication has always been the gospel's explosive superpower, capable of reaching the ends of the earth. You never know the eternal impact your words and actions will have.

I just received a newsletter from a student I discipled years ago with Cru. I remember the day she decided to make Jesus the Savior *and* Lord of her life. On a bench in Iowa City, we bowed our heads and prayed the most important prayer any person can lift up to God. She surrendered her whole self and future into the care of her Creator. Now, almost twenty years later, Ashley is on staff with a division of Cru, telling international students from all over the world about Jesus. She is discipling people into the kingdom. Who knows how many will be reached for Christ because of her willingness to be His messenger.

Spiritual multiplication is a holy domino effect that ripples into eternity. And in God's infinite wisdom, pouring into the few eventually reaches the many.

Looking at the Feet

While creation speaks of the glory and beauty of God, it is *we* who represent it. We are the ones charged with carrying the image and message of Christ as His ambassadors. Our specific purpose is different from the rest of creation because not only do we *show* people the truth and love of God, we *speak* it.

We are a masterpiece with a message.

Our invitation goes beyond "look at me" and says, "Come, let me tell you what God has done." No other created being can carry out what we've been called to do. Nature can point toward the goodness of our Maker, but it doesn't tell others how to know Him more. Only God's children can deliver the good news of Jesus Christ through the power of words.

We may have a multitude of goals and dreams, but our purpose will always end with bringing the gospel to those who need it (aka everyone). We can be go-getters, but unless we are gospel-givers we will miss the eternal impact God created us to have.

Paul says to the church in Thessalonica, "After all, what gives us hope and joy, and what will be our proud reward and crown as we stand before our Lord Jesus when he returns? It is you!" (1 Thess. 2:19). When others think about heaven, they often picture large mansions and crowns as a prize for following Christ. But here we see our reward is not found in possessions but *people*!

While thinking of those God has brought into our lives, who are ones we can pour into? Who is hungry for the seeds God wants us to plant? And will we choose to be dangerous to the enemy by being a daughter who is also a disciple?

Women who live according to Jesus' way care about the eternal destination of every soul. They are bold enough to say there's one path to everlasting life and His name is Jesus. They stay connected to Christ and teach others to do the same. They help the Bible be more a part of the church than culture is. They ask God for the opportunity to share their story and see Him answer that prayer.

Paul wrote one of the most eloquent and persuasive passages for being a Christ-centered disciple to the church in Rome.

> But how can they call on him to save them unless they believe in him? And how can they believe in him if they have never heard about him? And how can they hear about him unless someone tells them? And how will anyone go and tell them without being sent? That is why the Scriptures say, *"How beautiful are the feet of messengers who bring good news!"* (Rom. 10:14–15)

No matter where our lives land, we are sent to make way for the gospel message. Who knows what divine appointments and adventures

He has in store? Even if your skin is red and sweaty after running uphill in an airport to be Christ to a stranger, it'll be worth it. Our faces are radiant as we look to God, but they will never be as beautiful as our bold and willing feet.

If you would like to start a real relationship with Jesus and follow Him as a disciple, please read the prayer entitled "A Prayer for Becoming a Believer and Disciple of Christ" in the appendix!

Stories from Sisters Who Believed HE Could

TINA'S STORY:

A few years into my walk with Jesus, I sensed a barrier to the deepening of my faith. What began as an overwhelming desire to know Christ shifted into an apparent distance from the Lord with no real life to my faith. Despite my lack of enthusiasm during this season, I was compelled to read through the four gospels.

Within the pages of Matthew, Mark, Luke, and John, God revealed what had hindered my growth for so long—an old fear of offending others, which caused me to withhold from sharing the gospel. I was clutching my faith tightly to my chest, keeping its impact tucked within my own life, when God wanted me to extend the good news to others with open hands.

Over and over, the men and women touched by the grace and power of Jesus could not stay silent over what He'd done for them. Jesus never backed down from giving a bold witness to the truth of who He was or people's need to repent and believe for salvation. His mission to seek and save the lost would become every believer's mission, preaching the gospel to the ends of the earth and making disciples of all nations.

In this dark world full of despairing hearts, what a *gift* it is to share the good news with those around us. When we recognize we have an answer to the problem of evil and a hope that endures beyond the here and now—beyond a momentary pep talk or self-focused "inspiration"—we discern the immense opportunity available to us in every task, interaction, and aspect of our lives.

I admit it won't always be easy. But until the day I see my Savior's face, I cannot think of a greater sight than witnessing one of my children, a friend, or even a stranger take heart over a truth about Jesus I shared in word or deed. What a good God we serve, because the harvest of such blessing is available and abundant to all. (*Tina R. from Georgia*)

Chapter 10

HOW TO PUT THE ENEMY IN HIS PLACE (PART 1): UNDERSTANDING THE ENEMY

I remember the moment I saw evil face-to-face.

Freshly out of college, I was twenty-two, raising money to do full-time missions work wherever God would send me. That summer my parents and all five of us kids decided to vacation in Arizona. We said we were going to make memories, but in reality we were also trying to ease the stress in our family. One evening the relational tension hit a high note when fierce fighting erupted between everyone, especially with my youngest sister, Anna.

At the time, Anna didn't know she was worthy of love or acceptance from others, which made her react out of pain. The relationship between her and my parents was strained and suffering, and we all knew it.

After the yelling subsided and everyone was in bed, I went down to the living room where Anna was supposed to be sleeping on the pull-out couch. Her quiet sobs broke through the dark stillness in the room and my heart ached for her. I walked to the edge of her bed, sat down, and put my hand gently on her back as she continued to cry. I could see what was happening. The war within her was almost palpable. This was a battle for the life of my sister.

I began praying bold prayers, but not out loud, in hopes she would drift off to sleep. But something was different in that atmosphere. I couldn't shake the feeling someone was watching me. As my eyes scanned the shadowy room, I looked toward the patio door. What I saw made my heart stand still.

On the other side of the glass stood a hooded figure in black, his pale face staring at me. He was glaring with such disgust I could feel the extent of his hatred. This was no burglar disappointed he'd been discovered. This was something otherworldly.

Completely terrified, I froze, unable to look away or issue a single cry for help. Then I blinked, and in an instant, the looming figure before me disappeared into the night. He was gone or at least was out of physical sight. What I sensed that night seemed real, even if I was the only one who saw it.

To this day I believe only the Holy Spirit could have empowered me with the courage to rise and walk toward that patio door. I went straight to the spot where the hooded figure was standing and swiftly closed the blinds—in defense and defiance.

No one was going to mess with my sister. And no enemy is going to mess with my sisters in Christ today. Not if I have anything to say about it.

These next two chapters are probably some of the most crucial ones in this book because many are not aware or want to overlook this part of our spiritual lives. But there is an actual accuser roaming about, watching your comings and goings, doing his best to destroy your influence as a kingdom woman.

The Bible says, "Stay alert! Watch out for your great enemy, the devil. He prowls around like a roaring lion, looking for someone to devour" (1 Peter 5:8). Before a lion strikes, it stalks. It studies and listens. It watches and waits for the perfect moment to attack. Sometimes I wonder how long Satan watched Adam and Eve before he made his move. He was calculated and precise. He knew the exact question to ask that would make Eve question the character of God. Our enemy has perfected his evil craft and he, too, is on a mission.

Satan hates God. He hates love. He hates anything resembling goodness and kindness and truth. He hates the gospel and the fact that Jesus' death ushered in eternal life, which means the devil is ultimately defeated. And because you believe in Jesus and are filled with the Spirit of Christ, Satan hates you too.

Please know, I'm not saying these things to scare you. It's actually the opposite. I'm telling you these things in order to shine an unwanted spotlight on our enemy, which in turn will help us know who we are dealing with, reveal his hiding places, and thwart his plans. If we understand how Satan works, we will be empowered to put our enemy in his proper posture and place.

We Are at War Whether We Know It or Not

Sometimes when we hear the term *spiritual warfare*, we assume God is talking about someone else. We think it's not our territory, it's not our battle, and frankly, it's not our problem. But herein exists the lie. The truth is, if you are a believer in Jesus, you are automatically drafted into the war, even though the gospel guarantees our victory. Jim Logan, in his book *Reclaiming Surrendered Ground*, says, "Satan is defeated in the lives of believers only. He's got the unsaved world in his grip."[1] Logan goes on to remind us, "Being on the winning team doesn't mean you are excused from the battle."[2] Even though believers are on victory's side, we can still see and experience the effects of spiritual warfare. When we recognize the gravity of the situation, we will be more likely to fight for what's good. And when we decide to go to battle, we need to understand how to win the war.

We have a three-fledged attack occurring when it comes to resisting forces in our walk with God. First, we have the world and its unbiblical philosophies and agendas. A good chunk of this book has been spent (and will continue to be spent) dismantling the lies culture tries to feed to believing women. We are trading culture's lies for Christ-centered empowerment—an inferior form of liberty for the truth that sets us free.

Next on the list is our flesh. This is the innate part of us that daily needs to be crucified with Christ. Paul talked about the flesh when he wrote to the church in Galatia, "But I say, walk by the Spirit, and you will not gratify the desires of the flesh. For the desires of the flesh are against the Spirit, and the desires of the Spirit are against the flesh, for these are opposed to each other, to keep you from doing the things you want to do" (Gal. 5:16–17 ESV). Although we are new creations in Jesus and we want to be more like Him, we're also being made into the newness of Christ and need to surrender areas of ourselves that go against the Spirit's work. We are precious people in process.

The enemy likes to partner with our flesh by feeding its damaging desires, which will eventually lead to disaster or worse. Not every desire is a part of our flesh, however. Many desires are placed in our hearts by our kind King in order to bring about His purpose and glory. But if a desire goes against the Word, we can guarantee it's not a wise road to travel down.

And finally, as I demonstrated in the beginning of this chapter, we have our enemy and his roaming gang of demons who want nothing more than to stop the expansion of God's kingdom. The Bible says, "For we are not fighting against flesh-and-blood enemies, but against evil rulers and authorities of the unseen world, against mighty powers in this dark world, and against evil spirits in the heavenly places" (Eph. 6:12).

Have you ever wondered why epic movies and books involve evil battling good? It's because the battle is real! Warfare continually plays out in the unseen world as Satan goes after humanity, God's treasured image bearers, in an attempt to ruin the Father's plan. Unfortunately, Satan is pretty good at his job and shouldn't be underestimated, but we can learn how to understand his makeup and undo his twisted schemes.

Because this subject matter is so important, I want to spend not one but two chapters devoted to destroying the devil. The next chapter will dive into the practical and tangible ways we can come against Satan, but before we do that, like any good army general, we need to learn about our enemy because he sure knows a lot about us.

The Worst Kind of Enemy

Few people would choose to engage a charging army, but a visible attack is not the deadliest. The worst kind of enemy remains unseen. Satan is clever in that he does not want others to know he exists. Even most who participate in the religion of Satanism focus on being self-centered and worshiping themselves as the "god" of their own lives.[3] Satan doesn't want the credit for being the orchestrator of chaos, pain, division, death, and disease. *At least not yet.*

The devil's greatest goal is to blame humanity's Deliverer for all the destruction he's done. Satan wants to attribute his own toxic characteristics to the Trinity by accusing God for everything he destroys.

When trauma and tragedy strike, or heartache and hardship appear, the Creator is the one who is questioned. "Why did God do this? He must be cruel. How can a loving God do such a thing?" And yet, it is God who sits with us in our suffering and comforts our broken spirits. Jesus is the One who weeps with the children of the Most High. God's love and grace offer unending safety, security, and forgiveness, even when hard situations are allowed to happen. He cannot be anything other than good. It goes against His very nature.

Of course, the enemy wants us to blame our pain on the One who can bind up our wounds with His presence. Evil doesn't want us healed. He wants us hurting. By turning humanity's hearts away from the salve and salvation our souls need, Satan tries to make us reject God like he did (Gen. 3:4–5). He tries to make us suffer like he has . . . and will.

This battered world may be the enemy's playground, but earth is continuing to call for redemption and God hears the cries of creation. Suffering happens but the Savior promises to strengthen and support His own as the conquering Lion of Judah.

If Satan can't stop someone from blaming God or believing in Him, he'll try to make believers as ineffective as possible. The last thing the enemy wants is for people to become dedicated disciples of the living Christ. And trust me, he'll pull out all the stops.

He'll tempt us to remain comfortable in a lukewarm faith. He'll encourage us to fit in with the framework of society. He'll challenge us, attack us, and make us think we are too weak and worthless. He'll bombard Christ followers with lies and mislead them into accepting the term *inadequate* as a descriptor for their life. Meanwhile, Satan lurks in the shadows, glaring at God's children, hoping his maneuvers will stop them from recognizing who he is and how he works—all while making them forget or ignore who they are in Christ.

I'm a little too familiar with this common tactic. Satan tried to convince me to be an intentionally lukewarm believer.

For years I desperately tried to avoid standing out for Jesus. He was too taboo and too unsafe. His message was not trending in my circles, which meant talking about Jesus would not gain me popularity, and my people-pleasing heart couldn't handle it. I decided if I hid in the background and didn't talk about my faith, then others wouldn't reject me—at least not for that reason.

So instead of standing tall and standing up for my identity in Christ, I made myself small. I preferred being unseen rather than unliked. Thankfully, God used brave disciples in college to help rescue me from a track headed toward derailment. When Jesus woos us to Himself, He wants all of us so He can purposefully set us apart for the sake of the gospel.

Because you are reading this book, you too are choosing to stand out from society and stand against the enemy's lies dominating our culture. You are refusing to let Satan derail you from your sacred calling. You are choosing to rely on God instead of the self-powered philosophies originating from the one who first chose himself. And can I just let you know, God is saying "Well done!"

Many buy into a hurtful narrative that is distorted by the master deceiver. He makes bad appear good and right appear wrong. He leads people to believe finding freedom, peace, and happiness equates to doing what you want while being independent from God. But the opposite is true. Depending on God helps us avoid deception. Letting Christ love us helps highlight what's harming us.

The more time we spend getting to know God's personhood and listening to His gentle voice, the easier it will be to distinguish between the Lord and the liar.

Recognizing the Deceiver's Voice

We may not be able to see Satan, but we can certainly hear him. Have you ever been going about your day when, all of a sudden, negative self-talk takes over? Soon you are beating yourself up internally, and while you may think it came out of nowhere, think again.

Here's a simple example for you. I was driving my oldest to school the other day and his aide came out to meet us at the car. It was frigid because Midwest winters try to kill us summer-lovin' folk. While helping my son out of the car, David's aide lovingly took his hand and said, "Hey, buddy, do you have gloves?" It was an innocent question. She was thinking about his best and wanted to take care of him. But I was incredibly embarrassed. I forgot them at home, along with his hat. She was kind and said it might be good to have some at school just in case they went out for recess. I agreed, mustered up a half smile, and waved as I got in the car. Then I heard Satan's voice. "You are literally the *worst* mother. How could you forget something so obvious? They are going to think you don't take care of your children because, let's face it, you don't."

The enemy had been watching. He knew the struggles I had with feeling like a good mother for my kids, especially with David, who has special needs. He saw the perfect opportunity to jab at my core and gladly took it, over the simplest of mistakes. Unfortunately, the lie was effective because I listened to him.

After a couple hours fighting off shame, I recognized the accusations for what they were. *A load of tainted trash.* Like in the garden, Satan was trying to make me consume corrupt fruit. The Bible says the fruit of the Spirit is love, joy, peace, patience, kindness, goodness, faithfulness, gentleness, and self-control. But when the enemy speaks, his voice sounds like the inverse of these God-given fruits.

He'll replace love with *hate*, joy with *despair*, peace with *worry*, patience with *intolerance*, kindness with *cruelty*, goodness with *badness*, faithfulness with *faithlessness*, gentleness with *harshness*, and self-control with *selfishness*. If the voice we hear draws us toward any of these corrupt copies, we can send those accusations right back to the pit of hell.

Interestingly enough, his versions of the fruit of the Spirit are not the only fakes stored in Satan's reserves.

Don't Put *Satan*'s Armor On . . .

If you hang around Christians long enough, you will inevitably hear about the armor of God. I did a quick Google search for "armor of God study" online. Immediately, 11,500,000 results popped up. Clearly, the truths found in Ephesians 6 are an incredibly needed topic.

Not long ago, I had a horrible nightmare and was rehashing it with my husband. It seemed so real, I could feel fear building in my chest as I recounted its contents. But Madison said something that completely surprised me. After listening for a few minutes, he said, "Babe, don't put Satan's armor on." The phrase stopped me in my tracks. Was I doing that? Was that even possible?

I believe the answer is *yes.*

Satan and his wicked agenda are labeled the spirit of the Antichrist (1 John 4:3). Francis Frangipane, in his book *The Three Battlegrounds,* writes, "The spirit of Antichrist is simply that spirit which is anti-Christ! It is anti-love, anti-forgiveness, anti-reconciliation!"[4] Satan mocks and imitates any noble aspect related to the Godhead. He's called Lucifer, which means "bringer of light," a title he bore before his fall from heaven. Now, he is the bringer of darkness, which may appear as "light" to those who are unaware of its crooked source. It shouldn't surprise us that Satan has counter-Christ "armor" he wants to place on believers.

Except this armor doesn't keep people safe. It keeps people in bondage.

Armor provided by God is meant to empower His children to stand, but the enemy tries to replace God's protective covering with the opposite in hopes that they will collapse.

God gives us the belt of truth. The enemy offers the belt of deception.

Jesus supplies the breastplate of righteousness. Satan sends us the breastplate of shame.

The Spirit gives us shoes hemmed with the gospel of peace. Satan presents shoes weighed down with panic and fear.

The Father grants us the shield of faith in His ability. Satan gives us a shield of doubt in God's faithfulness.

The Lord hands us the helmet of salvation. The devil tempts us with the helmet of destruction.

God tells us to take up the sword of the Spirit, which is His very Word. The enemy wants us to wield hurtful weapons founded on foolish principles of this world.

Jesus directs us to pray and stand firm in His work. Satan wants us to strive to prove our worth, bypassing the victory we already have.

These two armors couldn't be more different. Life versus death. Freedom versus bondage. Faith versus unbelief. One armor is meant to defend; the other is meant to degrade. One armor is meant to protect; the other is meant to circumvent. Satan does not want us to become more like Christ. He wants us to become more like him, wearing the darkness he wears.

But we were made to wear the armor of God boldly. Unlike the enemy's counterfeit costume, God's armor is forged solely on what He gives us in Jesus. Satan wants us to look within to find the answers and authority he knows we cannot maintain on our own. The enemy is waiting for us to fail. Now we, as God's strong women, have to decide which set of armor we will wear each day.

If you are feeling discouraged in any way, remember, the gospel is always greater. The anti-Christ ways of the enemy do not stand a chance when we walk in our identity as the Father's daughters, even more so when we know how to take the snake down. The next chapter is going to offer the practical applications to do just that.

Let's get to work and take back some holy ground.

Stories from Sisters Who Believe HE Could

LAVONDA'S STORY:

It started as a day of celebration, my son's homecoming football game. Our son had gotten hurt and suddenly the day was filled with darkness. I found my heart weighed down by the heaviness of our hard situation. My legs were like wet spaghetti as I flopped into the hospital's waiting room chair.

I couldn't breathe. The room was spinning and stuffy like an attic that hadn't aired out for months. I finally stood up and knelt by the chair.

Then the voices started swarming through my head like annoying insects. "I'm going to take your son. You're a horrible mother. Why would you let him play football anyway, you idiot?"

And on and on the voices continued, resembling a broken record. I knew these were lies, but connecting my heart to my head seemed impossible. The Holy Spirit filled my heart with boldness and I rose up like a fearless warrior.

As I knelt in prayer, I envisioned the Lion of Judah urging me to safeguard its precious cub. It was time to battle. I got up quickly and began to speak the Word of God with power and authority over my son's life. He was in surgery with his future in jeopardy.

My prayer walk in the dimly lit hallways of the hospital ushered in the Father of light, and I pushed back against the present darkness. The same power that raised Lazarus from the dead was in me and I knew it. The atmosphere shifted as faith, hope, and love were restored.

I refused to allow strongholds of my past, such as unforgiveness and depression, to hinder God's purpose for me or my family. This injury was only a delay but it wasn't a denial; my son received healing.

The enemy may have power, but we are God's girls with authority in Jesus to take back our God-given destiny. (*LaVonda M. from Germany*)

Chapter 11

HOW TO PUT THE ENEMY IN HIS PLACE (PART 2): UNDOING THE ENEMY

Consider this chapter your armory and ammunition. Hopefully the previous chapter got your blood boiling a bit and also ignited a righteous anger inside as you thought about the ways Satan wants to treat God's children, including you. He doesn't want you to read what's laid out next.

We are going to dive right in and talk about the practices and applications we can add to our daily lives that will not only assist in undoing the enemy's schemes, but also cultivate a closer walk with Christ. Although we want to be aware of Satan, he is never to be the centerpiece of our faith. We fix our eyes on our Deliverer, not the demons who fear Him.

How about we start with the battleground in our hearts?

The Brave Work of Cleaning House

Some of the most powerful work done to put the enemy in his place doesn't involve focusing on the enemy at all. Confession, repentance, and forgiveness all encompass hard inner work that will eternally pay off. If we are willing to clean house for the sake of knowing Christ more intimately, then Jesus will make every inch of our hearts His home. And, in turn, our reflections will resemble more of Him.

Confession Creates Connection

Merriam-Webster defines *confess* as "to tell or make known (something, such as something wrong or damaging to oneself)."[1] When we confess something to God or people around us, we are lifting the veil and letting them see the reality behind the charade. We're revealing struggles we've intentionally buried, never knowing they would see the light of day. It's not easy confessing our struggles, even to the One who already knows every detail of our lives. Confession is courageous work. And it's also a pathway to freedom.

I have a vulnerable confession for you: I used to struggle with a sexual sin I barely told anyone about. I had concealed it for years because I didn't think it was something "big" that needed to be addressed. However, the effect of this sin was eating away at my spirit and hurting my relationship with my husband. One day the Holy Spirit made it clear I needed to confess my struggle to Madison. I felt nauseous for the rest of the day, palms sweating, doubts swirling, heart pounding. I almost copped out at the last second, but God gave me the strength to follow through and I reluctantly did.

To my amazement, my husband reached for my hand and told me he forgave me. Then, to further my amazement, he told me he had been struggling with the same thing. My obedience in confessing led us toward connection instead of conflict—first with God and then with each other. Was it easy? Not by a long shot. Was it worth it? Absolutely. While confession may have varying outcomes, bringing our sin into the light will help us experience a relief in our spirits and a fresh outpouring of God's grace.

What's interesting to me is how confession can fuel a sense of community if we let it. It's no wonder the devil wants us to remain quiet and hidden. "Me too" is a powerful statement, no matter what it refers to—something done to us, or something we've done or failed to do. It opens the door to true understanding and united compassion. Silence, on the other hand, leads to isolation, and the enemy is determined to make us feel alone and ashamed in our sin.

The enemy of our souls misleads us by telling us it's better to remain in darkness, but it's a message solely empowered by fear. When we worry about what others think, we forget God (the only One whose opinion counts) has already removed our sins as far as the east is from the west (Ps. 103:12). God made up His mind about us at the cross, covering our sins with no exceptions or fine print.

Paul wrote, "For God made Christ, who never sinned, to be the offering for our sin, so that we could be made right with God through Christ. As God's partners, we beg you not to accept this marvelous gift of God's kindness and then ignore it" (2 Cor. 5:21—6:1).

When we choose to avoid confession out of fear, we're also choosing to ignore God's mercy and the good news the gospel gives. And while nothing can separate us from God's love, we can make choices that prevent us from experiencing it in all its fullness. We can choose to avoid confession, even if it hurts us.

Don't play the enemy's game. You are God's child. You are a beloved saint who is not spiritually stained by sin. Rest in His love as you come boldly before the throne of grace and come clean to Him.

The Difference Between Confession and Repentance

While *confession* requires telling a truth, *repentance* involves a response to that truth. We confess with our words and repent with our actions. The two go hand in hand in our Christian journey. The day I confessed that deep-rooted sin to my husband, I asked God for the strength and self-control needed to change my behavior. Just saying *sorry* over and over wasn't going to cut it, even if I felt bad each time I apologized. I didn't want to remain the same, sitting in a continual pattern of pain. I wanted to turn away from the life I was leading and turn toward God's capacity to redeem.

In Hebrew the word *repent* is *teshuva,* which derives from a verb meaning "to return."[2] But what are we returning to? Estera Wieja, who is on staff with Fellowship of Israel Related Ministries, talks about repentance as an act of returning to our Father. "We get the order all wrong when we think the journey of repentance starts with fixing our mistakes before we can approach the Cross. What makes us capable of repentance is our belief that we belong to God and that's where we need to return."[3] Many get nervous when the word *repentance* is used, but if *returning to Jesus* is our focus, repentance is not something we need to dread. Instead, it's a practice we can openly welcome because we know God is standing there waiting to embrace us.

A key to being a woman of influence for the kingdom is being someone whose walk matches her talk. Hypocritical Christians have no lasting influence besides misrepresenting the character of God. We need to be authentic. We don't want to be women who shy away from real growth and change just because it may be uncomfortable. God has endowed His daughters with tenacity, a trait hemmed in for the long haul.

I'm thankful I didn't let the enemy get the best of me in my conversation with Madison. I now make it a regular habit to ask the Holy Spirit to reveal any areas of my life He wants to transform, knowing that repentance is an avenue leading toward restoration and a return to my faithful Father. Repentance ultimately leads us home.

Seeing Forgiveness as Our Friend

Sometimes I wish I wasn't as familiar with forgiveness as I am. God knows I've been through a fair share of relational heartache, including my relationship with myself.

In her book *Forgiving What You Can't Forget,* Lysa TerKeurst wrote, "Forgiveness isn't an act of my determination. Forgiveness is only made possible by my cooperation."[4] For a long time I believed I had to will myself into forgiving someone. I would try really hard to prevent bitterness from taking root. And while my intentions were good, the way I was choosing to forgive was empowered by myself, not by God.

Lysa's quote highlights how forgiveness is not dependent on us. It's a work of the Holy Spirit. Yes, we decide to start the forgiveness process by being open to God's healing work in our lives. But when we invite God's forgiveness to supernaturally flow through us, we become instruments of love in the hands of the One perfecting our faith.

The Bible draws a correlation between our realization of being forgiven and our ability to extend love to others. In Luke 7:47, Jesus addressed a woman whose sinful life made her come to the Messiah with overwhelming gratitude. She cried over His dirty feet, wiping them with her tears and hair. She kissed his feet, then anointed them with expensive perfume.

Jesus looked at Simon, a Pharisee in whose home they were eating. Simon thought Jesus shouldn't let this woman touch Him because of her impurity. And Jesus knew Simon's thoughts. He knew Simon compared himself to this woman who was lavishly loving Christ. Jesus taught Simon a lesson he wouldn't forget. "I tell you, her sins—and they are many—have been forgiven, so she has shown me much love. But a person who is forgiven little shows only little love."

What are the implications of such a statement, especially in the home of one who tries to follow the law as closely as he can?

Those who recognize they have been forgiven extravagantly will show love more extravagantly. If we take this a little further, those who understand God's undeserved forgiveness for themselves will be more likely to extend the same forgiveness to those who have hurt them. Or that's how it should be. Love and forgiveness cannot be separated from each other. If we want to show love to someone, we must choose the way of forgiveness.

God is our model, which means He goes before us, showing His children how to navigate rocky roads in relationships. Jesus paved the path to forgiveness through His death and resurrection, but also through His choice to offer forgiveness—not only to His friends, but to His enemies as well. C. S. Lewis says, "To be Christian means to forgive the inexcusable, because God has forgiven the inexcusable in you."[5]

In an ironic turn of events, sometimes our own worst enemy (besides the devil) is ourselves. Looking in the mirror and forgiving the person staring back is often more difficult than forgiving people who have hurt us, because we feel like *our* mistakes are inexcusable. We should know better. We should have learned this lesson by now . . .

But God has already established who can experience His forgiveness: those who freely receive Christ's work on their behalf.

Jesus' lesson to Simon is not meant to spur comparison between who has sinned more or less. Instead, the heart of God is to radically challenge our understanding regarding who and what can be forgiven when seen through the lens of the gospel. Everything and everyone can be forgiven, and that includes the often difficult task of accepting God's grace for ourselves.

These three practices—confession, repentance, and forgiveness—are game changers when applied to spiritual warfare. They are incredibly powerful and proactive in preventing the enemy from gaining a foothold in the first place. Ephesians 4:26–27 says, "And 'don't sin by letting anger control you.' Don't let the sun go down while you are still angry, for anger gives a foothold to the devil."

A foothold is maintaining a secure position but specifically "a firm basis for further progress or development."[6] Whatever we let into our hearts will help lead our feet. Depending on the posture of our hearts, we will progress one way or the other. If we are postured toward Jesus, we will progress toward life. If we are postured toward self, we will progress toward death.

Choosing to pursue confession, repentance, and forgiveness is not optional for our spiritual health. They are nonnegotiable, even if we don't feel ready to do the hard inner work. God loves us too much to leave us hurting or in sin. If we let our readiness be the gauge, our emotions will be the driving factor instead of the Holy Spirit. Satan wants us to wait, but God knows delaying is dangerous and it slows down our development and healing.

Wielding the Lethal 3: The Power of Prayer, Praise, and Proclaiming God's Word

Are you ready for another trio that will wreak major havoc on the kingdom of darkness? They all have to do with how we interact with God.

Not only does God give us the power to do all things through Christ, He also makes sure we are equipped with the right weapons that pack a holy punch. In 2 Corinthians 10:3–5, Paul wrote, "We are human, but we don't wage war as humans do. We use God's mighty weapons, not worldly weapons, to knock down the strongholds of human reasoning and to destroy false arguments. We destroy every proud obstacle that keeps people from knowing God. We capture their rebellious thoughts and teach them to obey Christ."

Through lethal spiritual weapons, we as God's daughters have the ability to tear down obstacles from Satan, society, and self. The enemy wants to get a *foothold,* but God offers us *strongholds.* A stronghold is defined as "a building or other structure that is safe from attack."[7]

Actually, the Bible uses this term in both positive and negative ways. Psalm 9:9 says, "The LORD is a stronghold for the oppressed, a stronghold in times of trouble" (ESV). The Lord is our steady stronghold meant to keep us safe in the battle.

The Bible also notes, however, that Satan creates strongholds. But these are more like barbed hooks or cold dungeons invading our lives (and the world) with the purpose of stopping kingdom work. He tries to keep us stuck behind walls of confusion and condemnation. He tries to keep us chained in worry and isolation. The walls of a stronghold originally meant to provide safety can, in the hands of our enemy, become a prison preventing us from experiencing freedom and goodness.

But God comes to the aid of His bride. He provides extremely effective weapons, all of which simultaneously take out the enemy and deepen our relationship with Jesus. We've likely participated in these three practices, but did you know they can also be used in times of war? Let me introduce you to the Lethal 3.

Prayer.

Praise.

Proclaiming God's Word.

The first weapon is one we may take for granted, but prayer is not something to be trifled with. It's a powerful part of our arsenal against enemy attacks.

The Powerhouse of Prayer

I've learned to pray for the people I'm thinking about when I wake up, first thing in the morning. Many times I don't remember my dreams, but usually if someone is brought to my mind, I've come to find they've been placed there by God. If our spirits never sleep, this is one way the Holy Spirit helps us pray without ceasing.

There's a reason Paul urges us to pray at all times in every occasion. Prayer is our ever-available lifeline that is connected to the concerns and care of others. The ripple effect of our prayers echoes into eternity, setting God's plan into motion, moving heaven and earth for the sake of His glory. God puts people, desires, and requests on our hearts intentionally in hopes that we may ask and He will answer. When we pray, we deepen our union with our Creator, but we're also calling for the Father's kingdom to come down. We may not always feel the power of prayer, but we will see its ripple effect in eternity.

Prayer is so important in our walk and warfare because it enables us to release what was never ours to carry. We have a Father who wants to hold our burdens *and* an enemy who wants to hinder us through burnout. Satan wants to keep us from the Burden Bearer. By presenting our requests to God, we claim Him as our protector and provider, instead of taking Satan's bait to wear the weight of our worries. "Don't worry about anything; instead, pray about everything. Tell God what you need, and thank him for all he has done. Then you will experience God's peace, which exceeds anything we can understand. His peace will guard your hearts and minds as you live in Christ Jesus" (Phil. 4:6–7). God wants to be our guard, but we need to give Him the opportunity to show us He can. We need to believe He wants all of our prayers, even the ones we'd never tell anyone else.

If you'd like to see how threatening something is to the devil, stand back and look at the attack. Satan wants to stop prayer, and his go-to tactic is primarily through distraction.

I could be mindlessly scrolling social media on my phone and it is calm in my house (calm being a *very* relative term in a boy-filled home). But the second I decide to pray for someone, especially my family, things go haywire! The phone rings. Multiple work emails come in. The dog pees on the floor. Some child tries to climb the cabinets. Meltdowns increase. And before I know it, I forget to pray and move on with our wild life.

It's no coincidence. The enemy will stop at nothing to keep us from praying. Why? The kingdom of darkness shakes when prayers from the saints are sent in Christ's name.

Never underestimate the power of your prayers or God's capacity to answer the cares you place before His throne. He is always listening and moving. God answers prayer and when He does, the brightness of God's glory will make the devil's dark deeds grow dim.

The Potency of Praise

I've had chronic pain in my abdomen for more than a decade, and after the thousandth medical test, the answer remained the same: "Everything looks good. Your results are normal."

While I was happy nothing serious was occurring in my body, I knew something was still not right. I couldn't sleep because of the discomfort. I couldn't do my regular activities. I could barely keep up with work responsibilities and helping run our special-needs home. I felt depleted, and discouragement began to give way to depression. I'd been through these cycles before.

What do we do when we are in these worn-thin spaces, unable to physically, emotionally, and mentally do what we think is needed?

This is when praise becomes a priority.

When we are thrashed about by our turbulent world and enemy, we wait for reprieve and restoration only God can bring. I believe this is what Paul was talking about when he said, "The Holy Spirit helps us in our weakness. For example, we don't know what God wants us to pray for. But the Holy Spirit prays for us with groanings that cannot be expressed in words. And the Father who knows all hearts knows what the Spirit is saying, for the Spirit pleads for us believers in harmony with God's own will" (Rom. 8:26–27).

What a testimony to a faithful God! Even in our weakest state, we can count on the Helper to help us reach out to Him. The Spirit speaks up for us, advocates for us, and defends us like a dear friend.

Sometimes we don't have the words to pray because we are barely surviving our day. But we don't need words when we can borrow songs from others who have gone before us, sisters and brothers who have poured out their hearts to the Father in praise. God wants us to use the weapon of worship.

We can lean on others' words when we don't have the ability to express our own. Listening and singing songs written by God's people helps us lift our heads high toward our real home. We remember who God is and what He promises. It allows our spirits to be softened in order for our Maker to nurture our souls.

It shouldn't surprise us that the book of Psalms is the source of many popular verses quoted when people go through difficult times. The psalms are songs written by musicians like David (75 of the 150 psalms are attributed to David) as God's people were being persecuted and experienced suffering. The authors were familiar with the power and perspective praise brings, how God's splendor can actually be seen in the sorrow. They knew a thankful heart was actually a worshiping heart and a worshiping heart was also a warring heart. David the psalmist was a writer, worshiper, and warrior.

Our enemy is very aware of this connection.

Satan was once an angel who stood in the presence of God. He beheld our majestic Maker receiving glory and praise, and pride churned deep inside, making Satan crave the same glory for himself. He wanted to be like God and steal what God alone could receive. Now, every time we praise God, Satan is reminded of the attention he still does not have. And it makes his evil heart cringe. Even as our praise angers the enemy, it also plunges a dagger of defeat into his evil belly.

I don't know about you, but I'm good with making the devil squirm. I think God's daughters should make it a regular practice to use the potency of praise to turn the devil and his demons away. When we praise God and thank Him for what He's done, we remind the enemy who he's messing with and who will ultimately win.

Because nobody can try to raise themselves above the Most High and live.

The Weight and Weapon of the Word

From the first moment Satan interacted with Eve, he distorted God's Word. This will always be the enemy's *modus operandi*. Why? Because if we don't know the truth, we can easily be misled down destructive paths.

You would think the enemy would use a different tactic when tempting the Son of God in the wilderness, but he doesn't. He tests Jesus who is called *the* Word, and tries to distort the meaning behind Scripture in order to make Jesus jump off a building!

> Then the devil took him to the holy city, Jerusalem, to the highest point of the Temple, and said, "If you are the Son of God, jump off! For the Scriptures say,
>
> 'He will order his angels to protect you.
> And they will hold you up with their hands
> so you won't even hurt your foot on a stone.'"
>
> Jesus responded, "The Scriptures also say, 'You must not test the Lord your God.'" (Matt. 4:5–7)

If Satan used Scripture against the Son of God as a means to destroy Him, he will have no problem doing the same with us. This is why being anchored in God's Word and declaring the truth is vital to standing strong against the enemy!

Does standing up to the enemy in warfare intimidate you? It doesn't need to. It's sobering because God has called us to battle and serious because souls are at stake. But God provides all the weaponry we need and the courage to wield it. We know that *He* can and *He* has and *He* will continue to do so until all evil is eradicated.

In all three instances when Satan attempted to make the Son of God sin, Jesus quoted Scripture back as His answer to temptation. That says something. It offers us an example worth emulating, a fellow soldier showing us how to defeat an enemy with whom He is more than familiar.

We talked about the armor of God in the previous chapter, but I wanted to make another important note. The sword of the Spirit, which is the Word of God, is the only offensive piece incorporated into the armor. Everything else is built for defense. Prayer and praise can also be used offensively, but wielding the Word cuts through the enemy's lies with force. It's sharp and effective. It draws the definitive line. The devil knows he can't win against the Word. That's why after hearing Jesus' scriptural rebuttal three times, the enemy retreated and left Jesus alone.

It's also the reason that this book is full of *biblical empowerment,* in order to fill your soul with truth and life. Based off of God Himself, our best means of disarming the enemy is to know and use His Word.

Hebrews 4:12 says, "For the word of God is alive and powerful. It is sharper than the sharpest two-edged sword, cutting between soul and spirit, between joint and marrow. It exposes our innermost thoughts and desires." The cutting process is usually not the comfiest. It can sting, even in our relationships, as we divide between what is right and wrong, what is true and false.

When you dissect something, it exposes what's really going on inside. You can't have a successful surgery without piercing through the surface. The same goes with our walks with God; we can't have a thriving relationship with our Maker if we don't let His truth enter and change our lives. The Word purifies and refines us. It renews our minds so we can be aligned with God's mission. It transforms thoughts, breaks patterns, and changes the trajectory of our course. As Christ said, the Word is the bread that sustains our hungry souls (Matt. 4:4).

In 2 Timothy, Paul wrote that all Scripture is inspired by God and is useful for teaching what is real in order to help us recognize what is false (2 Tim. 3:16). When studying counterfeit money, the banker first needs to meticulously study the genuine before being able to spot the fake.[8] Consistently instilling God's Word into our hearts and meditating on its truths are essential to combat a worldview constantly counterfeiting the gospel. False doctrines are fashioned in order to appease cultural philosophies and trends or to avoid stepping on toes. But if we soak in the truths of Scripture, any time lies are exposed we can stand our ground and dismiss them quickly.

It's important to note that immediately following Christ's testing in the wilderness, He began His public ministry and called His first disciples to follow Him. We are often brought into the still and surrendered places before God sends us out on missions. The Son experienced this preparation time, saturating Himself in the Father's love and truth.

According to 2 Timothy 3:17, Scripture is used to "prepare and equip his people to do every good work." Being grounded in the Word is a requirement if we want to represent Jesus well. We need our foundation firm because the enemy will try to shake up our circumstances, starting with our mindsets. He wants to prevent us from making an impact and spiritually multiplying God's kingdom through discipleship. But as we can see with Christ, the truth doesn't just set us free; it's also a weapon that makes the devil flee!

When Jesus rebuked the enemy with Scripture, Satan had to move on to the next tactic—until he eventually gave in and left. I've found it particularly effective in warfare or worry to proclaim God's promises out loud and pray verses over myself and my loved ones.

My husband and I have prayed for people as a team. God continually encourages me to read the Bible out loud over the person while Madison prays against the enemy. It's a double-edged sword, with the power to cast the enemy out and cut away toxic lies so wounds can finally mend. There are no better life-giving words than words authored by God.

Letting the Serpent Know Where You Stand

In the garden of Eden, after Adam and Eve ate the forbidden fruit, God told all parties involved about the consequences of their actions. But there's an important verse you can carry in your pocket and whip out any time you need to remember the power you have in Jesus. Instead of addressing Eve first, God directed His rebuke toward the serpent, a decision we should really notice. Clearly, God knew where the deception began.

He said to Satan, "And I will put enmity between you and the woman, and between your seed and her seed. He will crush your head, and you will strike his heel" (Gen. 3:15 BSB). One wound would sting, the other would be fatal. Even though the battle between humanity and the devil has been raging, God promised Eve that her offspring would ultimately crush the head of the one who deceived her. Eve's seed would slay the serpent.

This prophecy is about our Jesus—the Savior who shattered the enemy's plans and led God's family to triumph. Yes, His heel was struck on the cross, but His death made way for the devil's defeat, and Jesus' resurrection makes way for our rule with Him.

Brave friend, you have the authority in Christ to conquer Satan's schemes. You have access to all of God's arsenal, spiritual weapons that won't let you down. You have the right as a child of God to put the enemy in his rightful place. And I pray the flame to do so grows fiercer each day.

At Eve's lowest point, when the Father could have turned away, He chose to pursue her. God didn't discourage His daughter. *He empowered her.* He gave her hope for the future by promising her victory. Not by her efforts, but by the offering of her Seed.

So don't hold back or step away from the battle. Go ahead and put the enemy in his permanent place. Because Christ lives in us, we can crush the serpent's head in triumph too.

Stories from Sisters Who Believed HE Could

CHARITY'S STORY:

I didn't care if the drivers in the cars by me at the stoplight thought I was a lunatic, it was time to end the enemy's lies. Fighting against invisible, powerful forces I heard familiar lies. "You're alone. You don't deserve rescue."

I straightened my spine in defiance, pounded the steering wheel, and declared, "My Daddy owns the cattle on a thousand hills. The world and its fullness are His. God said He was going to pay my debt off, and He will do it!"

Peace saturated my body, heart, and mind. My overwhelming grad school debt remained, but I didn't feel the recurring shame over my debt.

I sped through the green light to get ready for my birthday dinner. Two years prior my dad had committed suicide. His loss stung on every level, but especially in moments when I felt lost.

"How do I get out of this mess?" I wondered. God kindly began to reveal Himself as a perfect Father who never fails and provides for us. I realized I was believing lies about who my Father God was. I believed He wouldn't provide for me because I'd made a mistake and I was destined to financial torment.

I repented for believing lies that were incongruent with the gospel. Jesus made a way for sinners; He gives undeserved grace and provides a pathway for our freedom.

Finishing birthday dessert, I was stunned to see fifty friends waiting with the birthday surprise of a lifetime: a giant check for the full amount of my debt, $43,333. Friends and family had secretly raised money for me.

While I had been fighting in the spiritual realm, rejecting lies and believing truth in my heart, God was working in the natural realm to release the provision I needed. All praise to our faithful Father. (*Charity R. from Texas*)

Chapter 12

WHAT TO DO WITH OUR GOD-GIVEN RIGHTS

This is the chapter I almost didn't write. Welcome.

When I initially brainstormed the topics for a book addressing Christian female empowerment, I knew the Lord wanted me to talk about our rights and choices. But not in the way you'd expect.

We make a lot of choices each day. *Psychology Today* estimated around 35,000 on average.[1] We can choose to love or hate, smile or frown, engage or disengage. I choose to step away from debates on social media because society is a hot mess of opinions and public slams. But, honestly, things don't look much different within the church.

The devil has planted division in the body of Christ by instigating fights over various spiritual issues. Satan works extra hard to make it seem like disagreeing with someone is the same as defriending them. Yet, when we look at the Bible, we see the disciples of Christ disagree about viewpoints, but remain connected as a spiritual family.

Although many believers aren't aligned perfectly on each issue, our faith in the gospel remains the unifying factor. Our example for the treatment of others, especially brothers or sisters in Christ, is based off the same Person. We can choose to emulate Jesus' character, even when we have conflicting views.

Christ shows us how to extend compassion and conviction in unison. He interacted with a world much like our own, full of strong opinions and objections opposing Scripture. If we ever wonder how to navigate Christian relationships or our heated culture, it's safe to follow the Son of God's choices.

What Was God's Choice?

Getting married was a hard transition for me, but nothing compares to the transition into motherhood. I never knew all my mom had done for me until God called me to do the same.

Motherhood is a life of sacrifice, service, and selflessness. It's the complete opposite of what the enemy would have us do. And so, when we found out our oldest son was autistic, I felt incredibly nervous and ill-equipped for the job. How could I meet his needs and help him thrive when I had no idea what I was doing? Could I lay down my expectations for the sake of embracing the life God wanted our family to have? It's been more than twelve years and the sanctifying journey continues. But the Lord, who is the perfect Father, showed me that all of parenthood comes down to a single choice.

Will we choose Christ-centered or self-centered love?

The Bible says we are called to love our neighbor as ourselves (see Matt. 22:39). Notice it doesn't say hate yourself, make sure to belittle your value, and never prioritize taking care of your overall health. If we want a healthy church, we need to make sure we are loving ourselves and others equally.

But the Bible does call us to a higher standard as disciples of Jesus. The passage prior to the famous "love your neighbor" verse highlights an important caveat that puts everything else into context.

The Pharisees approached Jesus, hoping to trap the Son of God in His words as a way to discredit Him. A lawyer who was also a Pharisee asked Jesus what the greatest commandment was in the Law. The Messiah saw what was happening and replied, "You shall love the Lord your God with all your heart and with all your soul and with all your mind. This is the great and first commandment" (Matt. 22:37–38 ESV).

And how do we love the Lord? Jesus answers this question in the gospel of John, saying, "If you love me, you will keep my commandments" (John 14:15 ESV). Love coincides with obedience. We can't say we love God with all of our hearts and refuse to do what He says. This is why when the Pharisees were asking Jesus which was the greatest commandment, He gave the wisest, most all-encompassing reply He could give. If we love God with all our hearts, we will obey what He says, even if it goes against what we want or the popular views of the world.

God always chooses love—to do what is right, holy, and good. And we are called to choose the same way of Jesus, despite its making us feel uncomfortable or uneasy.

What Does Christ-Centered Love Look Like?

If I could summarize the love of Christ in a single sentence, it would be this: *Jesus was humble.*

The bookends of Christ's life on earth were marked with humility. He was born in a manger near where dirty animals roamed and waste covered the ground. He was crucified on a cross where thieves were condemned and criminals were tortured. From the moment He was born until His dying breath, Jesus lived an intentionally humble life.

Paul described this intentionality in Philippians by saying, "Though he was in the form of God, [he] *did not count equality with God a thing to be grasped,* but *emptied himself,* by taking the form of a servant, being born in the likeness of men. And being found in human form, he *humbled himself by becoming obedient* to the point of death, even death on a cross" (Phil. 2:6–8 ESV).

I love the NLV's translation of verse 6: "Jesus has always been as God is. *But He did not hold to His rights as God.*" As women, our equal human rights have been withheld and dismissed for centuries. The discrimination and devaluing of women are undoubtedly wrong, and it's one of the reasons Jesus came to die—to reconcile and restore the ripple effect of sin. But as we will see in the next section, Satan has taken these cruelties and corrupted them even further with a cunning lie, making women focus on their rights to choose versus their rights as God's children.

The book of Philippians captures the essence of Christ's choice—*love for others over love for self.* Jesus chose to lay down His rights as God for humanity's sake. At any moment He could have said, "That's it. These people are rejecting Me left and right and don't see who I am or what I am doing for them." Instead, He chose to fulfill the work of the Father versus fueling the right to be offended. He decided to empty Himself by becoming a servant whose focus was the salvation of God's sacred image bearers. Jesus laid down His *rights* as well as His *life*.

Sisters, if we are to imitate Christ, *humility* is our God-given right.

Humility is the foundation for extending love to anyone. If we think we are better than someone else, we will find it hard to lovingly serve them. If we think we are correct and knowledgeable in all things, we will find it hard to listen and learn. If we think we are above reproach, we will find it hard to receive gracious correction or conviction from the Holy Spirit.

Jesus Christ is the most important person in history. He embodies wisdom itself. He is the pure and spotless Lamb, free from any blemish or sin. And yet, when Jesus interacted with others, He humbled Himself to let us see how God draws near to the broken and enters willingly into our pain.

Humility is a marker of strength that cannot be stolen. No matter what others say about us or how they may hurt us, humbling ourselves under God allows us to separate our worth and acceptance from the approval of man. You can't get much freer than that!

As much as is dependent on us, for the sake of the gospel we put aside our rights in order to point others to Jesus. This is not the most popular version of the gospel, but it is the biblical one.

The apostle Paul attempted to make something very clear to believers in Corinth. Although he had the right to be paid and supported by those he was ministering to, he chose not to. "What then is my pay?" the apostle asked. "It is the opportunity to preach the Good News without charging anyone. That's why I never demand my rights when I preach the Good News. Even though I am a free man with no master, I have become a slave to all people to bring many to Christ" (1 Cor. 9:18–19). Paul later said, "I try to find common ground with everyone, doing everything I can to save some. I do everything to spread the Good News and share in its blessings" (vv. 22–23).

The gospel compels us to sacrifice, serve, forgive, listen, and obey what God has commanded. And while it may not be convenient news, it is at the heart of the good news of Christ. If we combine the full idea of love—which includes obeying God's commands—with staying humble, our love will stand out like a beacon of light in a dimming, dying world.

Loving someone the way Christ loves us means recognizing the cost and still doing what is best or needed for the other. It is one of the most difficult decisions we need to make and it will determine how we represent Jesus in a God-adverse environment. People push back heavily when their rights are threatened, but our rights are not the focus in the gospel—*relationship is.*

With this being said, humility needs to be led by the Holy Spirit. Only God can help us find the balance of being kind and respectful of others' opinions, but also keeping our feet planted on truth.

Contrary to what culture believes, we can love someone and also disagree with them. Disagreement does not automatically imply dislike or division. Jesus told His disciples multiple times that the world's viewpoint will not be in line with the Word's. Humility acknowledges the importance and value in all people regardless of whether we agree. But being humble also requires submitting to the authority and knowledge of the Father, even if others come against us.

It takes resolution and resilience to be humble when hostility is present. Yet humility does not make a person weak, in the sense of being helpless or powerless. On the contrary, Jesus was humble but also the epitome of strength. He made Himself low and was forever lifted high. Even though He was humiliated publicly, He never lost His sense of sonship to the Father. Christ's focus was always heavenward.

We are called to be loving and lay our rights down for the sake of others, but we prioritize our relationship with God and His Word above all else.

We need to ask for the Lord's empowerment to practice true humility, which does not look like being a constant doormat. Instead, we are like doorways, highlighting the need for people to come to the Door, which is Christ Himself. Together we beckon others to open the door as they come in and receive the truth about Jesus and who they were created to be. We welcome others into the kingdom and, in turn, reap the blessings promised to the humble. Humility results in honor.

What Eve Alone Can Do

Yes, my friend, I'm going to go there.

In all honesty, I feel like I cannot talk about Christ-centered empowerment without touching on the topic of abortion. Satan has masterfully coupled the idea of women's rights to this practice, saying it represents empowerment. And for that, I would like the words I write next to take the venom out of his bite.

The devil has curated the lie that if you are a woman with a heart for empowerment, then you must also be a woman in support of abortion. My body. My rights. My choice. And yes, as humans we do have a choice because God offers us free will. But as believers in Jesus, our choice should align with God's will too.

I have no intention of shaming anyone who has had an abortion or telling you the vast number of babies whose lives have been lost. I know a great many women who have experienced this harsh procedure and I pray my words do not cause further pain. *My focus at this moment is to break the bond between women's rights and abortion.*

No matter what culture tells you, it is possible to be for female empowerment and also uphold the life of the unborn. They are not exclusive. In fact, from the beginning they were meant to coincide.

As we discussed in the previous section, our rights as children of God must fall under the umbrella of love and humility. We choose love over hate. Service over self. Life over death. But God also gives us a clue to the woman's critical role because of the title she is given.

Why do you think Adam chose to name the woman Eve? He could have chosen any word to describe who she was and what he perceived her to be. But Adam beckons to her essence, especially after the consequences of the fall were declared.

Up until they ate the fruit, the woman was not called Eve. She and Adam were referred to as man and woman. But immediately following God's judgment because of their disobedience, Adam turned to his wife and gave her a name.

She is called *Eve.* The Hebrew word meaning "*to live*" or "*life.*"[2]

The perfect timing of this naming does not get lost in translation for me. After humanity's decision brought sin and mortality into reality, Adam instantly yearned for life in the face of death. And then he saw his wife and remembered God's command to multiply and he realized hope is not lost! Eve would be able to play a crucial role in redeeming the effects of the curse. Essentially, Adam was thinking, "All we see is death, but God enabled her to bring life!"

Genesis says, "The man called his wife's name Eve, because she was the mother of all living" (Gen. 3:20 ESV). The term *Adam* was used to generally describe humankind. But woman needed a separate name. She could do something reserved by God only for her.

Yes, God is the author of life and men are needed to procreate, but Eve is His carrier, bringing forth fellow image bearers into physical existence. Eve cocreates with the Creator by developing and delivering life into this world.

Only Eve can do this. No man can do what she can do.

God has sacredly chosen us as women to be instruments of life in a world obsessed with destruction and death. And Satan knew this. He knew the power and potency of women and viciously tried to wipe God's vessel out through the fateful fruit. In hopes of killing Adam and Eve, the serpent lied to the woman, convinced the man to go along, and tried to prevent her offspring from happening. (Cain and Abel anyone?) He went after Eve and her family *hard*.

Right from the moment the serpent is cursed in Eden, there is rising tension between Satan (who has the power to destroy) and Eve (who has the power to create life). "I will put enmity between you and the woman, and between your offspring and her offspring; he shall bruise your head, and you shall bruise his heel" (Gen. 3:15 ESV). God's redemption plan can be seen in this verse with Jesus coming from Eve's distant offspring and His victory over Satan on the cross. Yes, Christ's heel was bruised, but Satan's head is the one that is crushed.

The enemy's hostility toward Eve grew even more when she started to undo his schemes by partnering with God to cocreate life. And so, Satan has cleverly switched up his game, and we see it played out perfectly when looking at female empowerment today.

What better way to corrupt Eve's essence and accomplish his

horrific schemes than to get Eve to *partner with him instead*?!

Women have been deceived by the serpent once more.

Right now, he whispers, *Did God really deem you Eve? Wouldn't you rather choose your life instead?* Such temptation is hard to resist if our eyes are not fixed on God's Word.

Satan wants to empower women by encouraging them to look toward self. Christ wants to empower us by pointing toward sacrifice.

Jesus told His disciples shortly before His death, "This is my commandment: Love each other in the same way I have loved you. There is no greater love than to lay down one's life for one's friends. You are my friends if you do what I command" (John 15:12–14).

Any woman who has given birth can tell you this is true. When you give birth, you are literally laying down your life for the sake of not only a friend, but your child. You are choosing love at all costs. I have never been closer to death than when in labor with my oldest.

After a day of intense labor and pushing, I felt my body give up. I looked at my husband and uttered, "I'm done." I knew I barely had any life left in me, certainly not enough to push out a child. My vitals were dropping, as well as our baby's. The room instantly turned into an emergency situation. I vaguely remember signing a paper holding the hospital harmless of the responsibility for my death if that should happen. They rolled me to the operating room and within thirty minutes our son was born. It was such a blur and I'm grateful for the small recollections of seeing our boy's face for the first time. It was worth it, but I have never been closer to meeting Jesus.

Ultimately, there are two lives at stake when a woman is pregnant and both are equally important to their Maker. When we think about our God-given rights, we must think about Jesus and the way He handled privileges that were due to His name. We must think about the way He commands us to love.

Christ thought of us. He served His family. He sacrificed willingly, knowing the cost would be worth it. He chose to instill life through His very death. No greater love, my friend.

And no greater example for Eve—and us—to follow.

What to Do with the Rights God Gives

So now what? If we know who we are and we embrace the essence of Eve, how do we practically play this out each day?

For starters, it's important to remember women bring life into this world in various ways, not just through childbearing. I have dear friends who long to be mothers but because of infertility or other life circumstances they cannot physically bring babies into the world. And yet, they certainly are Eve.

When a woman is empowered by Christ, she takes the life-giving aroma of the gospel everywhere she goes. She walks in her identity as a woman fully alive and free. As her feet touch the ground, she makes her Father smile and her enemy shiver.

Regardless of whether she has physical children or not, when a woman pours her life into others, she builds up the family of God through her words and deeds. She is a mother to those living in Christ and a minister to those who are lost. Every woman is Eve.

Next, as God's family it is our job to provide a safe and caring community for expecting mothers and their families, regardless of whether a pregnancy is planned or unexpected. Often when women experience unplanned pregnancies, their hearts are filled with a plethora of emotions and concerns. Pressure, fear, shame, and confusion crowd a woman's heart when she is at the crossroads of deciding what to do.

This is when the church needs to step up. We need people whose passion for the mothers, as well as the unborn, moves them to take action. We need more Christ followers willing to grab the trembling hands of women and assure them they will not walk this hard journey alone. Christ-centered fellowship should also go beyond birth and stretch into the season of motherhood.

Amy Ford, the founder of Embrace Grace, started an international organization devoted to equipping churches so they can give pregnant women needed support and care. They empower women to choose life by being pro-love. Amy says, "We can't just vote a certain way or talk about what needs to change, we *are* the change."[3] I highly recommend checking out their website and buying Amy's book, *Help Her Be Brave*, for more ways to be an agent of change and healing in the lives of unexpectedly pregnant women.

Although the church is continuing to awaken to its call to look after women experiencing unplanned pregnancies, God's family is often not the safest place for women in these situations to land. Instead of welcome, they receive rebuke. Ford emphasizes,

> Shame doesn't make someone want to do the right thing. It makes people want to run away, hide, and isolate. But God's love doesn't work that way. It is a magnet that pulls hearts toward Him. No one can conceive life without the consent of God, the author of life. The baby is not a sin. A baby is a miracle. All lives, no matter how they got here, should be celebrated.[4]

Rejecting the mother also means rejecting the baby. But we, as followers of Jesus, worship a God who pursues the frightened, vulnerable, and lost. As the body of Christ, we need to do better. *Much* better.

Even if our church is not yet empowering women with unplanned pregnancies, we can provide a gracious covering in the form of comfort and compassion. Kind words and deeds are meant to extend beyond the pews. If you ask God, He will cause your path to intersect with those who need the open arms of Christ. Then, it is our choice if we will love them toward life.

Finally, there are earthly rights like fighting to end injustices done against women and standing up for fair treatment in society. These battles are not only good but biblical. But if we are focusing on what has been given to us by God, we need to remember *our rights must line up with what's righteous in order to be a right of the kingdom.*

If culture's man-made rights do not line up with the truth found in Scripture and the Father's definition of love, then they are not rights we should fight for.

Displaying the Rights of the Kingdom

I know I've talked a lot about the sacrifices we make as servants of Jesus, but there are real benefits to being a child of God.

When we trade our human rights for heavenly rights, we inherit the everlasting rights to God's kingdom. As His children, we have the gift of an eternal and intimate relationship with our Savior. We have the right to abundant life for God's glory. We have access to every spiritual blessing in Christ. We have the right to suffer with Jesus but also to be filled with joy, love, kindness, and other aspects of the fruit of the Holy Spirit. We have the right to dominion and authority over evil and sin. We have the right to proclaim Christ's victory and praise His matchless name. We have the right to shine Light into an ever-darkening world.

Recent studies have shown when a sperm meets an egg at fertilization, zinc sparks fly, which produces a microscopic flash of light.[5] In a beautiful way, conception retells God's first recorded words in the process of creation. "Then God said, 'Let there be light,' and there was light. And God saw that the light was good. Then he separated the light from the darkness" (Gen. 1:3–4).

From the moment we come into existence we are called to be bearers of Light. We illuminate what God says is good and true. We are the daughters who honor and uphold the way that leads to life. I pray our generation will be bold enough to proclaim the excellencies of Him who called us out of darkness into the light of what's humble and right.

Stories from Sisters Who Believed HE Could

REBEKAH'S STORY:

As I reflect on the two miscarriages I've endured, one occurred during the first trimester, the other during the second. I remember the emotional suffering and grief I experienced and am still navigating after their deaths. The lives I had once carried inside of me invoked biological changes that my body responded to, changes in hormones defined as postpartum. For many women, postpartum can cause depression and anxiety, even with their baby at home in their arms. For those who do not bring their baby home, this can cause deep emotional suffering.

The truth is, we were designed to miss our babies. The Creator intentionally made us that way. It's how mothers are able to go to great lengths and do whatever is necessary to take care of their children. Would my body still go through postpartum changes if I removed the value that was placed on my babies' lives? If I didn't desire to have them in the first place, does that dismiss what my body was designed to do?

Our society has come to believe a detrimental lie. Women may believe our souls can walk away unharmed from making the choice to end life inside of our wombs, but our biological makeup says otherwise. Not only will our bodies respond the way all women's bodies will when death occurs inside of them (with waves of emotional grief), but our souls will yearn and ache for life.

Abortion brings death to the most vulnerable part of our

body—our womb. Our Creator designed women to carry life, not death. It's why for both the bereaved mother and the post-abortion mom there's great suffering and understandable pain. Only God has the authority to place value on human life. He is also the only One who can bring healing balm to our hearts for both. (*Rebekah B. from Kentucky*)

Chapter 13

CULTIVATING HOLY COURAGE IN A HARSH WORLD

I was four months pregnant with our youngest son when the deer ran in front of my car. Pregnancy cravings were getting the best of me and I was returning home from a late-night run for crazy bread from Little Caesars. Butter and garlic, my friend. Need I say more?

Home was three minutes away. My neighborhood was in sight. I gazed around at the roads and thanked God they were not covered in ice, a common occurrence for Midwest winters.

One second later the buck smashed violently into the passenger side of my car. The whirl of motion forced a frantic scream out of me, although I barely realized what was happening. I swerved the car, but the buck had already done its damage and disappeared.

My body was shaking uncontrollably as I turned into the first street possible and stopped the car. Reaching down to touch my belly, I prayed our baby boy was okay. *Please God, don't let any harm come to our son.*

With fumbling fingers, I managed to call my husband.

It was only after I stepped out of the car that I saw the aftermath of the accident. Through a haze of hot tears, I saw that half of our minivan's front bumper was crushed inward, leaving a gaping, smoking hole. It was a miracle I wasn't bruised or hurt.

My husband picked up his phone.

"Babe," I said as I began to sob. "I just hit a deer." My fast breathing produced a heavy fog that filled the night air with fear.

"Are you okay?! Are you hurt? I'm heading out the door now."

In a matter of minutes Madison arrived and our evening plans shifted from laying low to filing police reports and calling in insurance claims. The police never found the deer that left a significant impact on my car and, more potently, *me*. Both the baby and I were fine physically, but I was jolted mentally and emotionally. The constant replay of the accident haunted my mind and dreams. A running list of "what-ifs" continued to grow as I obsessed over what might have been.

What if it was worse?

What if we lost our baby?

What if I didn't survive?

What would happen to my family?

The hypotheticals went from being perturbing to paralyzing. Not only did this incident come close to claiming my life, it almost stole my child's too. While I tried to not think about the accident, it affected me to my core and made me not want to drive again for weeks.

Once again, I discovered that life is fragile. It's a reality we all come to know. No matter how much we try to plan or strain for control, everything changes in an instant when hardships crash into our lives.

Sometimes we see the coming collisions in the distance. We sense something is off and scan the harsh landscape, hoping we can do anything to avoid the situation or pain. We know it's probably going to take more than we can give. And so, we prepare. We process. We pray.

Other times, life smashes into us at unprecedented speeds. We don't expect the loss. We didn't want the change. We can't believe the diagnosis. We don't know how we are going to make it or make do with the heartache that's been handed to us. Difficulty forces us to pivot without warning or welcome.

It doesn't matter how pain collides with our plans; the fact is, each one of us encounters a world with an uncanny and unpredictable mix of beauty and burdens. The confusing combination can foster fear, convincing us to hide and bury deep any bit of courage the Lord has placed in our hearts.

It's hard to get back behind the wheel when we know what's out there. After walking the path of grief or experiencing the terrain of suffering, we can't go back to how life was, but how do we face the life we now live?

A famous verse in the Bible tells us to be "strong and courageous" in the midst of life's trials (Joshua 1:9). And yet, courage is often born out of fear. Fear of the unknown. Fear of failure. Fear of rejection. Fear of loss. Fear of the worst happening. But in the second half of this popular verse we see how being near to Jesus gives us the strength and courage to press on. "For the Lord your God is with you wherever you go."

Being brave, it would seem, has much less to do with us being without fear and more with us having faith in the One who is by our side. If courage isn't solely dependent on us, but we are called to be courageous, it makes us ask an honest question: What does biblical courage really look like?

Cultivating Biblical Courage

Culture's definition of courage is simple—*we are self-made brave!* When fear comes knocking, we put on the bravest of faces and pull up those big girl panties. We face the fear, even if we're scared, in order to show everyone (including ourselves) we are strong and can conquer anything. This mindset sounds empowering and, dare I say, almost achievable, except for two facts.

(1) Our own courage can only take us so far.

(2) The concept of courage never started with us.

If we believe we are made in the image of God, we must also believe we have aspects of God's character etched into our being. We have a holy DNA, as I like to call it, that reflects who the Creator really is. But just like anything resembling love, goodness, or kindness in this universe, showing courage is only possible because we have God's nature running through our veins. Without God, there would be no bravery. All of creation would live in a constant state of fear if God hadn't instilled this concept in our souls first. God is our source of courage.

Once we become a child of God, courage is amped up to a new level. We are now empowered to be courageous in Christ. Not only is courage part of us, now it can flow through us. God's Spirit gives us the strength to move forward, even if we're scared.

Many times we can feel fearful when we are required to do brave things. The main characters of the Bible were commonly scared when God called them to do His will. Moses, Jonah, Esther, Isaiah, Elijah, Hagar, David, Gideon, and the original disciples are some of the top contenders. But God had these characters covered, and He continues to offer a covering for us today.

I host a weekly series on my website called the Brave Women Series and the idea of "doing it scared" comes up often. But being empowered by Christ's courage is more than doing it scared. Instead of striving to produce our own bucket of courage, we can borrow some from Him.

God has carried out the most courageous acts we can think of. Loving others when you know they will reject you? Check. Laying down your life for your friends? Check. Pursuing wayward children? Check. Washing the feet of our enemies? Check. Forgiving the worst of offenses? Check. Standing up for others? Check. Preaching the truth? Check. The Lord's cup of courage runneth over. Although we may wonder if *we* are really brave, remembering we are empowered in Christ helps us recall *who* makes us brave.

The Bible assures us we don't need to face our fears alone, hoping our courage can bring us through, because in the long run, it can't. What we can do is ask Jesus for some of His, knowing God does not call us to be courageous on our own.

It's important to note, God does not ask us to be fearless in order to take steps forward. All He asks of His followers is that we trust and obey. God will take care of the rest. Putting our faith in the ability of our Father means we don't need to be perfect regarding our emotions. Fear can originate from a variety of sources. It can be a natural response to difficulty, an attack from the enemy, a response to our own sinful choices, or even a result of our unbelief in the character of God. But feeling fear is not always a sin. What we do with our fear, however, makes a real difference in our walk with God.

Taking our fears to the feet of Jesus is the most freeing thing we can do for our hearts. Only then can He wash us in His Word and show us He is worthy of our trust. Even if we don't know what's ahead, as we get to know the care of our Savior, our faith becomes rooted in Him.

The apostle Paul listed three words together in the book of 1 Corinthians, stating that this trio will last longer than any other gift we receive from God, besides Himself. *Faith. Hope. Love* (1 Cor. 13:13). Not surprisingly, they are connected in the concept of courage too.

Love is the foundational reason God promises to be with us throughout trauma, tragedy, and trials. We can trust the Lord's heart for us. This helps cultivate biblical courage in Christ and His power to make all things right. But the final word I want to spend the rest of our time focusing on is hope. Having faith in our loving God brings about a communal element of hope for the end of our stories.

Cultivating Christ-Centered Hope

As believers, we can face heartache differently than those who do not know God because we know how the story unfolds. We've read the final chapter. We know we are on the winning team. Like Christ, we can endure hardship and pain for the joy set before us in heaven.

The author of the book of Hebrews wrote,

> Therefore, since *we are surrounded by so great a cloud of witnesses,* let us also lay aside every weight, and sin which clings so closely, and let us run with endurance the race that is set before us, *looking to Jesus,* the founder and perfecter of our faith, *who for the joy that was set before him* endured the cross, despising the shame, and is seated at the right hand of the throne of God.
>
> Consider him who endured from sinners such hostility against himself, so that you may not grow weary or fainthearted. (Heb. 12:1–3 ESV)

We are surrounded by many witnesses who endured and persevered in our fallen world, and these people are more than those listed in the book of Hebrews' hall of faith. We are in the company of friends, family, and brothers and sisters in Christ who understand how to hold hope and hardship in their hands at the same time. Still, it's easy to focus our eyes on the harsh conditions we find ourselves in, when in reality our eyes should be fixed on the King sitting on the throne.

In the final book of the Bible, Revelation, the apostle John described the throne of God. "And He who was sitting was like a jasper stone and a sardius in appearance; and *there was a rainbow around the throne,* like an emerald in appearance" (Rev. 4:3 NASB).

Can I tell you about rainbows for a second? God used this glorious arching bow as a sign of the covenant He made with Noah to never again destroy the earth with a flood. A covenant is the most sacred form of a promise. And when God makes the covenant, it cannot be broken because He would be denying His very nature—His trustworthiness, His power, His faithfulness. He would be denying Himself. When the Creator makes a covenant, it cannot be changed.

Back to rainbows. I found out recently that the rainbows we see today, which are the same as the days of Noah, are only a fragment of the whole picture. Rainbows, as it turns out, are not arched bows but full circles!

According to meteorologists, rainbows are full circles that can only be seen from the air or a higher perspective.[1] On the ground, however, from our everyday viewpoint, we can only see the arches as they stretch from one side of the horizon to the other. We see in part what God sees in full.

Right before Paul talked about faith, hope, and love in 1 Corinthians he said, "*Now we see things imperfectly,* like puzzling reflections in a mirror, but then we will see everything with perfect clarity. *All that I know now is partial and incomplete,* but then *I will know everything completely, just as God now knows me completely*" (1 Cor. 13:12).

The full glory of what God has promised is still veiled to us. We cannot see it or comprehend it quite yet, but one day we will. One day we will stand in the midst of this vast number of sisters and brothers in Christ and we will witness the Lord fulfill His promises in ways we could never imagine. The praise coming from our lips will echo on and never fade.

Just because we can't see the end . . .

Just because we can only comprehend in part what is happening in our lives . . .

Just because some of God's promises seem hidden or lost . . .

It does not mean His promises are not fully there. We just can't see them yet.

God graciously formed the rainbow into an infinite circle, symbolizing how His promises have no expiration or end. He understands the pain and grief we tread through on earth. Jesus walked the path to one of the most gruesome deaths invented while experiencing constant persecution and rejection, even from His closest friends. But because we have a steadfast hope in what's to come, we can see life's trials through the lens of our Savior.

Like Jesus, we can let Satan know the damage he's done will not outdo the splendor to come. We can persevere through present hardships because we know there's a permanent hope for our future. The eternal scale will always be tipped in our favor.

One day we will live in paradise in our unbreakable bodies. We will stand in the presence of the Most High and worship our Lord, who is the King of glory. This doesn't make our earthly suffering any less sorrowful, but it does cultivate in us a strong and, dare I say, defiant hope that resembles Christ's. "For our present troubles are small and won't last very long. Yet they produce for us a glory that vastly outweighs them and will last forever!" (2 Cor. 4:17).

Hope does not disappoint, my friend, because heaven's perspective tells the final story.

A Final Prayer and Commission from Christ

There is a glory coming too marvelous to understand, but we can experience the glory of God right now. We have the opportunity to share the goodness of gospel-centered living and its ability to reframe and change our lives. If you're like me, you may have heard how Jesus promoted the upside-down kingdom of God. But I am starting to see things in a different light.

As Kristi McLelland wrote in her study *Jesus & Women*, "Jesus did not come to turn things upside down. Jesus came to turn things right side up."[2] Jesus came to rescue us from the ruins of sin. He came to set things straight, as they were always meant to be. He came to bring us back to Eden, but this time as conquering daughters in Christ.

Jesus chose to go against what many were expecting of Him. The masses thought the Messiah would lead a revolution to overtake Rome. Instead, Christ led a revival in the hearts of humanity that reconciled the lost to God. Today, He invites us to participate in that same revival—a Christ-centered revolution pointing people toward a *Person*, not a supreme power or privilege. This is our greatest commission.

There's no greater calling, which will require all the courage Christ gives.

Standing strong for God will not be easy, especially when the current of culture is flowing fiercely in the opposite direction. On top of the difficulties we will experience in life, Jesus demonstrated firsthand how following the Father guarantees rough reactions from the world. Unlike the prosperity preachers of our day, Christ promises pushback. He promises opposition. Jesus let us know we would attract those who are leaning toward life and repel those directing their decisions toward death.

Paul wrote, "Our lives are a Christ-like fragrance rising up to God. But *this fragrance is perceived differently by those who are being saved and by those who are perishing.* To those who are perishing, we are a dreadful smell of death and doom. But to those who are being saved, we are a *life-giving perfume.* And who is adequate for such a task as this?" (2 Cor. 2:15–16).

I can tell you who is adequate according to God: you! He has been in the business of equipping and empowering you, even before you were born.

Did you know Jesus prayed for you? In John 17, Christ prayed to the Father for His disciples, just before His crucifixion. I think it is fitting to end this book with the last prayer Jesus prayed for His disciples—*the words He also prayed for us.*

> I have given them your word. And *the world hates them because they do not belong to the world,* just as I do not belong to the world. I'm not asking you to take them out of the world, but to *keep them safe from the evil one.* They do not belong to this world any more than I do. Make them *holy by your truth; teach them your word, which is truth.* Just as you sent me into the world, *I am sending them into the world.* And *I give myself as a holy sacrifice for them* so they can *be made holy by your truth.*
>
> I am praying not only for these disciples but also *for all who will ever believe in me* through their message. (John 17:14–20)

We do not belong to this temporary world; we belong to Jesus. We are women who are being made holy by clinging to God's truth. Even when society scorns us or others treat us harshly, we know it's because we bear the name of Christ.

May we bear it boldly.

Our Savior loves us and has prayed for us to stand firm in the way of His Word. He blesses us with eternal promises and will be faithful as we put our confidence in His covenants.

Together with Jesus we can win the battle against culture's lies and prevail over the serpent's schemes.

Christ has been empowering Eve since she took her first breath, and now He is sending us out into this hungry world in order to highlight the One who will save it. We are the brave women proclaiming the freedom of the gospel.

We believe our God can.

Now, let's go and do.

Stories from Sisters Who Believed HE Could

BEKAH'S STORY:

It was November of 2016. We lived in SoCal at the time, so flowers were still blooming, as they do year-round there. My brother-in-law tapped on the back patio door to get my attention. As I moved toward the door, I saw a grin on his face, pointing to a pot in his hand. I looked down to see him holding a ridiculously beautiful yet broken flower. It was firmly planted in a terra-cotta pot and had grown full and yellow, but endured some damage midway up the stem to the point where it was nearly cut in half. The flower itself hung low, blooming courageously on a stem held together by mere threads.

I stood speechless because this was a literal image God gave me more than a year before. I had drawn this broken and beautifully blooming flower in my journal, a symbol for my own life.

My boys had been diagnosed with a rare and fatal disease when God gave me this image. I could not save them. In the middle of devastation and damage to my own little world, God reminded me that we are connected to the Vine. And as I experienced holy courage that only He could supply to my humble branch, God lifted my eyes to His victory. His redemption. His trustworthiness. His goodness. His hope. "Remain in me," He whispered. "Stay connected."

As I stared at that flower, I knew before me was a road to a different kind of bravery. A full surrender to the way of this Vine was the holy courage I needed to thrive in this world. And as Jesus rooted and firmed up my foundation, the Spirit flooded nutrients into my grief-filled heartbreak, where God met me with such kindness and produced hope.

Friend, no matter what you face today, connect to the Vine. This is the only way to holy courage as we walk these broken, but oh so beautifully redemptive, paths. (*Bekah B. from Idaho*)

Appendix

Discussion Questions for Book Chapters

Chapter 1: ~~You Are Enough~~ You're Not Enough, and That's the Good News

1. What is your definition of being "enough"?

2. How have you felt like you are not enough?

3. Do you have any hesitations admitting you are not enough on your own? Why do you think this may be the case?

4. How has shame or fear tried to prevent you from experiencing the good news?

5. How has the enemy deceived you into reaching for something other than Christ?

6. In what ways have you seen culture's message of empowerment affect your life?

7. What would it look like to allow God to be the Savior of your story instead of yourself?

8. Which truth from God's Word helps you let go of the impossible standard of being enough?

Chapter 2: ~~You Can Do Hard Things~~ You Can Do Hard Things the Easier Way

1. How have you tried to make things happen, even with pushback? How did you feel during the process?

2. What is your opinion of the phrase *God will never give you more than you can handle*?

3. What situations in your life seem like they are too much to endure?

4. How have you seen God show up in your weaknesses?

5. Is there something you are doing that God may want you to lay down? If so, what is it?

6. Which boundaries can you set in order to stop overcommitment? What is God directing you to do?

7. How can you ask God to help you step away from the pressure to perform?

8. Which hardships in your life has God used to help you rely on Him and grow your roots in Christ?

Chapter 3: ~~You Be You~~ You Be His

1. How have you tried to be someone you're not?

2. In what ways do you compare yourself to other women?

3. What are some negative things other voices, including your own, have said that are opposed to your identity in Christ? What is the truth you can claim against them?

4. How can you celebrate the way you and other women in your life have been made by God?

5. How does the fact that you are a child of God change the way you view others' opinions?

6. Has God given you any passions, desires, or skills that make you come alive? What are they? How are you nurturing your God-given gifts?

7. How can you ditch the perfection mindset today? What does God say about being perfect?

Chapter 4: ~~Believe in Yourself~~ Believe in Your God

1. What are some "only God" moments in your life?

2. Who are you depending on to work out the miracles, as well as the everyday moments, in your life?

3. How can letting go of control be an avenue of freedom in Christ?

4. In what areas can you be diligent and dependent on God at the same time?

5. How can you back your belief in God with your behavior today?

6. Have you ever been told you do not have enough faith? How did you feel, and how can relying on God's faithfulness help break off any shame?

7. In what way can you live with surrendered faith in God's sovereignty?

Chapter 5:
~~Speak Your Truth~~
Share Your Story, but Speak THE Truth

1. How has sharing parts of your story created a space for connection and community with others?

2. Why does sharing your truth versus sharing *the* truth matter?

3. In what ways can you communicate the truth with love?

4. What biblical truths are hard for you to communicate to others? Why?

5. How can you use your story to display God's truth?

6. How have you experienced healing because you have held tight to God's truth?

7. Who is someone you can pray for so they can see how the gospel can set them free?

Chapter 6: ~~Follow Your Heart~~ Follow Your King

1. Have you ever been told you are sensitive? How does your mindset shift to know God desires your whole heart, including your emotions?

2. How have you (or others) undervalued the importance of emotions in your walk with God?

3. What does it mean to guard your heart versus follow your heart?

4. In what ways have you seen the "follow your heart" mentality lead you or others down a destructive path? Do you believe God's main desire is for us to be happy?

5. What can you learn from the life of David about following your heart?

6. What longings of your heart can you entrust to Jesus today?

7. How can we choose to live with a heart devoted to Christ instead of a divided heart that follows culture?

Chapter 7:
~~The Future Is Female~~
The Future Is Found Together

1. How have you seen the attack on marriages play out?

2. How does a biblical definition of "helper" as "lifesaver" or a warrior change your view of the importance of Eve?

3. In what ways has Satan prompted women and men to fight against each other instead of fighting against the enemy?

4. Has anyone told you that you were less than because you are a woman? How does God view you instead?

5. What are character traits of a biblical leader? How does Jesus expect leaders to serve those He entrusts to them?

6. How can unity win the war in regard to male/female relationships? In what ways can we pursue unity, not divisive debates?

7. How can diversity and our unique makeup be a blessing to each other and the church?

Chapter 8:
You Can Slay All Day

1. Do you believe the same power that rested on the original disciples rests on you? Why or why not?

2. Have you ever diminished the power of the Holy Spirit out of fear or confusion? If yes, how?

3. Do you ever find yourself prioritizing different spiritual gifts over others? What does the Bible say about the different gifts of the Spirit and how valuable they each are?

4. In what ways are you trying to maintain control and slay in your own strength?

5. What are some tangible ways you can practice abiding in Christ today?

6. How have you seen the Holy Spirit empower you to do the impossible?

7. How does knowing you are secure and sealed by the Holy Spirit change the way you approach hardships in life?

Chapter 9: We Are Women of the Way: Spreading the Gospel Like Jesus

1. Are there any statistics about those who call themselves Christians that concern you? Which ones?

2. How would you define being a Christian? How does Jesus define a true believer?

3. What is the difference between claiming Jesus as your Savior versus making Him your Lord?

4. What characteristics are found in a disciple of Christ?

5. Who can you ask to disciple you, and whom can you disciple in order to build up the kingdom?

6. How can you live as a messenger of the good news today? Who can you tell about Jesus and the good things He has done in your life?

7. What kind of fruit (cultivation of your character) do you see God producing in your life?

Chapter 10: How to Put the Enemy in His Place (Part 1): Understanding the Enemy

1. What has been your opinion of Satan?

2. How does it make you feel to know you are in a war?

3. Have you experienced spiritual warfare, and what did it look like?

4. In what ways has Satan tried to get you to question the goodness and faithfulness of God?

5. What are some things you've heard the enemy say about you or your loved ones? What are the truths that can combat those lies?

6. What pieces of the enemy's armor have you put on instead of the armor of God? What should you replace it with?

7. How willing are you to step onto the battlefield? Who can you ask to pray for your spiritual protection as you do?

Chapter 11: How to Put the Enemy in His Place (Part 2): Undoing the Enemy

1. Is there anything you need to confess today to a fellow believer and to God?

2. How does viewing repentance as a return to God change the way you approach practicing repentance?

3. Who in your life do you need to forgive in order to avoid the foothold of bitterness or resentment? Is there anyone you need to ask for forgiveness?

4. Why is prayer so important in our walk with God?

5. How have you seen God answer prayer?

6. How has praising God helped you in times of pain or hardship?

7. In what ways can you practice consistently being in God's Word? And what verses can you pray over your life and over the lives of those you love?

Chapter 12: What to Do with Our God-Given Rights

1. How can we show compassion and conviction at the same time like Jesus?

2. In what ways has your obedience to Jesus shown your love for Him?

3. How does humility being our God-given right change everything?

4. What is one way you've put aside your "rights" in order to show someone Jesus?

5. Does the idea of sacrifice or humility imply weakness? Do you think Jesus lived His life with service and strength?

6. How can you lay down your rights for someone who needs it?

7. In what ways are you being Eve (bringing life) right now to those around you? All women embody Eve!

8. How does the essence of Eve affect the way you see the life of the unborn? How does it fight the lie the enemy is telling to women regarding abortion?

9. How can God use you to empower the church to help women with unexpected pregnancies?

Chapter 13:
Cultivating Holy Courage in a Harsh World

1. Do you believe you are brave? What does the Bible and God say about how you have been made for courage?

2. What circumstances in your life have tried to take away the courage God has given you?

3. Can you be fearful and brave at the same time? Why or why not?

4. Do you think fear is a sin? How can we avoid feeling shame if we are scared?

5. What fears do you need to take to the feet of Jesus right now?

6. How can living with hope help us be courageous?

7. What promise are you believing God for right now that you don't see fulfilled yet? What verse can you memorize to help you cling to the hope of what's to come?

8. What aspect of Christ's prayer for you stands out and ministers to your heart?

A Prayer for Becoming a Believer and Disciple of Christ

If you want to make a commitment to follow Jesus the way disciples of Christ did in the Bible, I would love to have you read the following prayer out loud (or in your head if you can't at the moment). Many people say they are Christians, but they are only comfortable accepting Jesus as the Savior of their life and not their Lord. Making Jesus the Savior of your life means you recognize the basic tenets of the gospel. . . . You're a sinner, someone who isn't perfect and never can be on your own. You recognize you need someone to pay the price for your sins because the wages of sin (as we have seen in Eden) is death—both physically and spiritually. We are separated from God because of our sin and nothing we can do will ever earn our way back to God because we are sinners by nature. God is perfect, good, and holy, and therefore needs a perfect, good, and holy sacrifice to forever pay for man's sins. Because no person can attain this standard, God sent His own Son, Jesus Christ, to be the payment for our sin by dying on a Roman cross. It was a death meant for us but a sacrifice God chose to make in order to have us with Him for eternity. He values our restored relationship that much! Jesus rose from the grave three days after His death, defeating sin and Satan, and His resurrected life makes it possible for us to have new life by believing in Him and what He has done. This invitation is open to all.

We can believe these things, but the Bible says, "If you openly declare that *Jesus is Lord* and believe in your heart that God raised him from the dead, you will be saved" (Rom. 10:9). It's not enough to just "believe" these things. The enemy and his demons believe Jesus died and rose from the grave. We must also confess Him as Lord, meaning we give Him the reins and right to our life. We do not keep living for ourselves; we live for Christ and let Him change us and mold us into imitations of Himself. We choose to obey His commands out of gratefulness and love. We let God make us into reflections of Jesus and we allow the Holy Spirit to sanctify us so we act, think, and love in the manner of God. If this is something you are ready to do, it's the most important and *best* decision you will ever make. It would be my honor to help you walk into a true relationship with Christ. Just read the prayer below . . .

"Jesus, I thank You for dying on the cross for my sins and choices. You are the only One who is perfect and therefore are the only One who could be the perfect and holy sacrifice for everyone's sins. Thank You for paying the highest price for me, for taking my place, because of Your extravagant love. I praise You for making a way for a restored and reconciled relationship with God. I receive Your gift of salvation by grace and faith alone, not by anything I have done. I repent of living according to my own desires and plans. I do not want to live for me anymore. I want to live for You because of who You

are and what You've done for me. I want to come back to You—to return home. I choose to believe in Your saving grace, Jesus Christ, and accept You as my Savior.

I also choose to submit my entire life to You. I surrender to You and give You control of my future and every moment of my day. I let go of the way I've been living and I choose to make You the Lord of my life. I confess You as both my Savior and my Lord. Come into my life and make me into the person You have created me to be. Help me know You more deeply and transform my mind and heart so they match Yours. I choose to be Your disciple and thank You for the gift of an eternal relationship together.

In Jesus' name I pray.

Amen."

Acknowledgments

Writing a book is not only a labor of love, it's a labor of long-suffering commitment, growth, and patience. It's a communal effort, and without the people listed below, I couldn't have done this.

First, I need to praise my grace-giving, empowering God. You are the reason I wrote this book. You are the One who brought it through the valley to completion. It's always been You. The way You radically transformed my life is a testimony to Your capability, character, and care. I only pray this book will help others experience the same freedom, love, and growth I have. Thank You for choosing me to be Your daughter and disciple. You are my everything.

Next, to my husband, the sacrifices, time, prayers, support, and copious amounts of chocolate you've given me throughout this entire writing journey have been my glue. God has used you to empower me in too many ways to count. You've held me, cried with me, fought for me, rejoiced with me, and have been my closest friend. Thank you for believing in the calling God has on my life to disciple and pour into women. Even more, thank you for being my partner in carrying it out. I couldn't have launched into this writing adventure without you. And to think it all started with "Grandpa's gnarly fingers." Ha! I love you always.

To my three sons who constantly remind me that God answers prayers and gives blessings beyond anything we could imagine, you keep me pursuing Jesus and praising Him for the gift of you. I love you, my treasures. Thank you for giving up mommy time in order for me to get the words on these pages. I wouldn't trade being your mama for anything in the world. I'm so proud of the young men of God you are becoming. You are my sunshine.

To my mom and dad, you have always encouraged me to pursue the dreams God has given me and to never doubt in the darkness what God has shown me in the light. Your love and support have been my backbone since childhood and now you are my biggest cheerleaders. Thank you for showing me what a genuine walk with Jesus looks like and for continually pointing me back to Him. God is faithful, and He has used your faithfulness to change my life. The reality of this book is in large part because of you.

To my siblings—Emily, Teresa, Anna, and Adam: your prayers, honest conversations, and encouragement have aided in holding my head high when I wanted to throw in the towel. Thank you for faithfully standing in my corner, but also for believing in me and giving me the grace to be myself while navigating through every season. God has used your love and compassion to show me the heartbeat of our Savior. I couldn't ask for better family and best friends.

To my extended family, thank you for being a voice of grace and truth that has steered me toward Christ. I'm truly grateful for how you've rallied behind me and believed in what God is doing. Gramma Joy and Grandpa Great, your steadfast love, prayers, and kindness have been such an anchor for me in rough and calm waters. I'm so glad Jesus brought you both into my life when I needed it most. You are the most wonderful, giving people.

To my dear friends who have been my bold prayer warriors, holding my hands up when I didn't have the strength, you are absolute joys to my heart and life-givers to my soul. Jenny, Andrea, Marnie, Pamela, Twyla, Sarah, Jodi, Susan, Casey, Jenni, Ashley, Donna, just to name a few—you all have cried with me, listened to me, inspired me, celebrated with me, emboldened me, battled with me, and sharpened me. I'm blessed to have the dream team of ladies championing this God-given dream. You are women who believe God can, and I'm incredibly thankful to do life with you.

To the amazing contributors in this book, thank you for saying yes and sharing your Christ-centered stories with us. I can only imagine how God is going to use the authentic words He inspired you to write. I admire, respect, and love you all.

To my fellow writers in Books & Such, Hope*writers, Compel, and beyond, thank you for being in this with me. Only writers fully understand the demands of body, heart, mind, and spirit when we write. Thank you for your insight, encouragement, and support since my beginning blog days. You helped me believe I was a writer whose words could be used by God to make an eternal difference, and you've helped me keep moving forward with Christ as my guide. I'm forever grateful for the friendships and community I've experienced.

To the women who have shared their stories in the Brave Women Series, your words have inspired me to be courageous in pursuing the publishing of this book. Thank you for partnering with me to help bring God's faithfulness, truth, and loving empowerment into our hurting world. You help make me brave.

To my precious community of brothers and sisters in North Carolina, your example of kindness, unity, and humility are transformative in my walk with Jesus. I'm so grateful God gave us another family when we moved from Illinois and that He chose you to stand beside me as I launch this book into the world! I love each of you.

To my literary agency, Books & Such, thank you for taking me on as one of your own and collectively championing this project. But particularly to my one-of-a-kind agent, Cynthia—what would I do without your expertise, advice, laugh, and friendship? Since the beginning of our relationship, you've made me feel like the most important client (even though I know you do this with every one of your clients!). Thank you for taking my hand when I was nervous, confused, and completely overwhelmed with parts of the book writing process. You have a shepherd's heart that looks out for those God has entrusted to your care, and you do it so well. I'm blessed the Jesus in me connected with the Jesus in you.

To my Moody editors and the entire publishing team, thank you for being brave and taking a risk on me. Trillia, thank you for believing in the message of this book and for helping bring it into fruition. Catherine, thank you for fielding my thousands of questions as a newbie author. Your grace and wisdom have been deeply appreciated repeatedly. Cheryl, I'm grateful for your sharp editing skills that helped make this book the best that it can be. I am honored Moody Publishers is standing behind the message of this book. What a privilege it is to create with you.

To my professors at Moody Theological Seminary, thank you for teaching me how to read the Word of God with wisdom, discernment, and the Holy Spirit's guidance. The lessons I learned from my graduate work in your classes have stuck with me and impacted my life as well as the expression of biblical truth in this book. You are continuing to leave a Christ-honoring legacy.

To the staff, volunteers, and fellow students who God used to transform me through Cru, you probably have no idea the difference you've made in my life. Chip, Lisa, Adrienne, Katie, Erin, Kristin, Katie, Becky, Charity, and many more, thank you for helping me recognize my identity as God's daughter for the first time. Your investment in me helped me see my call to ministry, my heart for sharing the gospel, and the true satisfaction that comes from being a disciple of Christ.

To Mr. Marvel and Mrs. Lillian, of all the pastors and people who poured into me as a young lady, I treasure you the most. You both played a big part in helping me understand the truths of the gospel and why I needed to live my life according to my beliefs. I will always remember your love for our Savior and your faithfulness to serve Him no matter what. Thank you for reminding me about the plans God has for my life and the hopeful future we have in Him.

To the endorsers of this book, thank you for your YES and your trusted backing of this book. Your kind words are so valuable to me and help me have confidence to say, "Let's do this!"

To you, the woman reading these words, thank you for trusting me enough to let the message of *She Believed HE Could, So She Did* become part of your journey with God. I thought of you the entire time while writing, and I'll continue to pray for you after the last page is read. God can and will empower you to change the world for Christ.

Notes

Introduction: How Can Female Empowerment Start with a Man?

1. James A. Borland, "How Jesus Viewed and Valued Women," Crossway, March 8, 2017, https://www.crossway.org/articles/how-jesus-viewed-and-valued-women/.

Chapter 1: ~~You Are Enough~~ You're Not Enough, and That's the Good News

1. "Gospel," *Encyclopædia Britannica,* https://www.britannica.com/topic/Gospel-New-Testament.
2. John Eldredge and Stasi Eldredge, *Captivating: Unveiling the Mystery of a Woman's Soul* (Nashville: Thomas Nelson, 2021), 84.
3. Ibid., 85.
4. *Cambridge English Dictionary,* s.v. "enough (*adv.*)," https://dictionary.cambridge.org/us/dictionary/english/enough.
5. *Merriam-Webster,* s.v. "enough (*adv.*)," https://www.merriam-webster.com/dictionary/enough.
6. *Merriam-Webster,* s.v. "empowerment (*n.*)," https://www.merriam-webster.com/dictionary/empowerment.

Chapter 2: ~~You Can Do Hard Things~~ You Can Do Hard Things the Easier Way

1. Dennis Merritt Jones, "Strong Winds Strong Roots: What Trees Teach Us About Life," *Natural Awakenings,* March 31, 2015, https://www.naturalawakenings.com/2015/03/31/274262/strong-winds-strong-roots-what-trees-teach-us-about-life.

Chapter 3: ~~You Be You~~ You Be His

1. *Merriam-Webster*, s.v. "hearing (*n.*)," https://www.merriam-webster.com/dictionary/hearing.
2. John R. W. Stott, "'In Christ': The Meaning and Implications of the Gospel of Jesus Christ," C. S. Lewis Institute, June 3, 2007, https://www.cslewisinstitute.org/resources/in-christ-the-meaning-and-implications-of-the-gospel-of-jesus-christ/.

Chapter 4: ~~Believe in Yourself~~ Believe in Your God

1. Tony Evans, "God Is Your Source—Tony Evans Motivational Moment," YouTube, June 3, 2022, https://www.youtube.com/watch?v=LMlLI9XUa10.
2. Attributed to Sir Francis Bacon in his *Meditationes Sacræ* (1597).
3. Sally Lloyd-Jones, "Believing and Doubting," in *Thoughts to Make Your Heart Sing* (Grand Rapids, MI: Zonderkidz, 2021), 126–27.

Chapter 5: ~~Speak Your Truth~~ Share Your Story, but Speak THE Truth

1. "Understanding Consent," NOMORE.org, November 25, 2022, https://nomore.org/learn/understanding-consent/.
2. Christopher Klein, "Why Did Pontius Pilate Have Jesus Executed?," History.com, March 27, 2023, https://www.history.com/news/why-pontius-pilate-executed-jesus.
3. J. I. Packer, *A Quest for Godliness: The Puritan Vision of the Christian Life* (Wheaton, IL: Crossway, 1990), 126.

Chapter 6: ~~Follow Your Heart~~ Follow Your King

1. Elaine Aron, "The Highly Sensitive Person," https://hsperson.com/.
2. Ellie Holcomb, *Fighting Words: 100 Days of Speaking Truth into the Darkness* (Nashville: B&H Publishing Group, 2021), 71.
3. A. B. Simpson, "June 16: 'Ye Cannot Serve God and Mammon' (Matt. vi. 24)," in *Days of Heaven Upon Earth*, https://biblehub.com/library/simpson/days_of_heaven_upon_earth_/index.html.

Chapter 7: ~~The Future Is Female~~ The Future Is Found Together

1. "Ezer Kenegdo," Wild at Heart, November 3, 2022, https://wildat heart.org/daily-reading/ezer-kenegdo.
2. Sandra Glahn, "What Does It Mean That Woman Is 'Helper' (Ezer)?," Bible.org Blogs, August 25, 2020, https://blogs.bible.org/what-does-it-mean-that-woman-is-helper-ezer/.
3. Eli Lizorkin-Eyzenberg, "The Unlikely Role of the Biblical Woman," Israel Bible Weekly, July 6, 2022, https://weekly.israelbiblecenter .com/the-unlikely-role-of-a-biblical-woman/.
4. Michelle Lee-Barnewall, "Ministry, Part 2: Rethinking Authority and Leadership in the Body of Christ," in *Neither Complementarian nor Egalitarian: A Kingdom Corrective to the Evangelical Gender Debate* (Grand Rapids, MI: Baker Academic, 2016), 113.
5. Lynn H. Cohick, "Priscilla and Aquila," Bible Odyssey, February 28, 2023, https://www.bibleodyssey.org/places/related-articles/priscilla-and-aquila/.
6. Mimi Haddad, "Priscilla, Author of the Epistle to the Hebrews?," CBE International, January 31, 1993, https://www.cbeinternational .org/resource/priscilla-author-epistle-hebrews/.

Chapter 8: You Can Slay All Day

1. "What Is Water?," American Museum of Natural History, https://www.amnh.org/explore/ology/water/what-is-water.
2. "What Is the Meaning of the Greek Word Dunamis in the Bible?," CompellingTruth.org, https://www.compellingtruth.org/dunamis-meaning.html.
3. Ibid.
4. Erik Raymond, "What Does It Mean to Be Sealed with the Holy Spirit?," The Gospel Coalition, September 17, 2019, https://www .thegospelcoalition.org/blogs/erik-raymond/mean-sealed-holy-spirit/.

Chapter 9: We Are Women of the Way: Spreading the Gospel Like Jesus

1. Gregory A. Smith, "About Three-in-Ten US Adults Are Now Religiously Unaffiliated," Pew Research Center's Religion & Public Life Project, December 14, 2021, https://www.pewresearch.org/religion/2021/12/14/about-three-in-ten-u-s-adults-are-now-religiously-unaffiliated/.
2. Michael Gryboski, "Only 6% of Americans Have a 'Biblical Worldview,' Research from George Barna Finds," *The Christian Post*, May 26, 2021, https://www.christianpost.com/news/only-6-of-americans-have-a-biblical-worldview-survey.html.
3. Tracy F. Munsil, "Basic Biblical Beliefs Lacking Among Most Pastors in All U.S. Denominations, All Church Roles," Arizona Christian University, August 30, 2022, https://www.arizonachristian.edu/2022/08/30/basic-biblical-beliefs-lacking-among-most-pastors-in-all-u-s-denominations/.
4. Tracy F. Munsil, "New Study Shows Shocking Lack of Biblical Worldview Among American Pastors," Arizona Christian University, May 12,2022,https://www.arizonachristian.edu/2022/05/12/shocking-lack-of-biblical-worldview-among-american-pastors/.
5. George Barna, "America's Dominant Worldview Syncretism," American Worldview Inventory 2021, Arizona Christian University, April 13, 2021, https://www.arizonachristian.edu/wp-content/uploads/2021/05/CRC_AWVI2021_Release01_Digital_01_20210413.pdf.
6. "St. Augustine of Hippo (About 354–430 AD)," Catholic Faith and Reason, https://www.catholicfaithandreason.org/st-augustine-of-hippo-about-354-430-ad.html.
7. Barna, "America's Dominant Worldview Syncretism."
8. "Where the Word 'Christian' Really Comes From," *Relevant*, September12,2022,https://relevantmagazine.com/faith/where-christian-name-really-came/.
9. Ibid.

Chapter 10: How to Put the Enemy in His Place (Part 1): Understanding the Enemy

1. Jim Logan, *Reclaiming Surrendered Ground: Protecting Your Family from Spiritual Attacks* (Chicago: Moody, 1995), 165.
2. Ibid.
3. Joe Carter, "9 Things You Should Know About Modern Satanism," The Gospel Coalition, October 23, 2019, https://www.thegospelcoalition.org/article/9-things-you-should-know-about-modern-satanism/.
4. Francis Frangipane, *The Three Battlegrounds: An In-Depth View of the Three Arenas of Spiritual Warfare: The Mind, the Church and the Heavenly Places* (Cedar Rapids, IA: Arrow Publications, 1989), 102.

Chapter 11: How to Put the Enemy in His Place (Part 2): Undoing the Enemy

1. *Merriam-Webster*, s.v. "confess (*v.*)," https://www.merriam-webster.com/dictionary/confess.
2. Estera Wieja, "What Did Jesus Mean by Repent? The Hebrew Meaning of Teshuva," FIRM Israel, August 3, 2021, https://firmisrael.org/learn/what-did-jesus-mean-by-repent-the-hebrew-meaning-of-teshuva/.
3. Ibid.
4. Lysa TerKeurst, *Forgiving What You Can't Forget: Discover How to Move On, Make Peace with Painful Memories, and Create a Life That's Beautiful Again* (Nashville: Nelson Books, 2020), 7.
5. "Reflections: The Necessity of Forgiveness," C. S. Lewis Institute, January 1, 2007, https://www.cslewisinstitute.org/resources/reflections-january-2007/.
6. Dictionary.com, s.v. "foothold (*n.*)," https://www.dictionary.com/browse/foothold.
7. Vocabulary.com, s.v. "stronghold (*n.*)," https://www.vocabulary.com/dictionary/stronghold.
8. Tim Challies, "Counterfeit Detection (Part 1)," Tim Challies, June 27, 2006, https://www.challies.com/articles/counterfeit-detection-part-1/.

Chapter 12: What to Do with Our God-Given Rights

1. Eva M. Krockow, "How Many Decisions Do We Make Each Day?," *Psychology Today*, September 27, 2018, https://www.psychologytoday.com/us/blog/stretching-theory/201809/how-many-decisions-do-we-make-each-day.
2. Eli Lizorkin-Eyzenberg, "What Does Eve Mean in Hebrew?," *Israel Bible Weekly*, March 8, 2023, https://weekly.israelbiblecenter.com/eve-mean-hebrew/.
3. Amy Ford, *Help Her Be Brave: Discover Your Place in the Pro-Life Movement* (Chicago: Moody, 2021), 17.
4. Ibid., 60.
5. Jillian Bell, "Fertilized Human Egg Emits Microscopic Flash of Light," CBCnews, April 27, 2016, https://www.cbc.ca/news/science/sperm-egg-zinc-sparks-1.3553550.

Chapter 13: Cultivating Holy Courage in a Harsh World

1. "Rainbow," National Geographic Education, https://education.nationalgeographic.org/resource/rainbow.
2. Kristi McLelland, "Jesus and Women in the First-Century World," in *Jesus & Women: In the First Century and Now* (Nashville: Lifeway Press, 2022), 33.